'Living in the age of the mobile phone, internet cafés and on-line shopping must mean living better, not faster. Duncan's light-hearted but provocative insight gives us 120 positive ways to achieve this. This is a must for those wanting to engage with the issues surrounding living in the twenty-first century.'

STEVE CHALKE, *OASIS TRUST*

'With its sporting stories and analogies, this little book will prove to be a great resource in my work with professional footballers. The bite-size pieces mean it can be read by anyone in a spare moment; yet its clever and creative style means it will be remembered long after breakfast time has finished. Reading one page leaves you hungry for more and more and more.'

GRAHAM DANIELS, *CHRISTIANS IN SPORT*

'There are some ideas I wished I'd had first. *Breakfast with God* is definitely one of them. A brilliant read, and especially for anyone who loves collecting good quotes.'

JOEL EDWARDS, *THE EVANGELICAL ALLIANCE*

'*Breakfast with God* is chunky for chompin' on — so eat it, baby.'

DAWNIE REYNOLDS, *SOUL SURVIVOR*

Breakfast with God

Duncan Banks

Marshall Pickering
An imprint of HarperCollinsPublishers

Marshall Pickering is an imprint of
HarperCollins*Religious*
part of HarperCollins*Publishers*
77-85 Fulham Palace Road, London W6 8JB
www.christian-publishing.com

First published in Great Britain in 2000 by Marshall Pickering

Unless otherwise indicated, scripture quotations are taken from the
Contemporary English Version Bible, © American Bible Society 1991, 1992, 1995.

1 3 5 7 9 10 8 6 4 2

Copyright © 2000 Duncan Banks

Duncan Banks asserts the moral right to be identified as the authors of this work.

A catalogue record for this book is available from the British Library.

ISBN 0 551 03250 2

Printed and bound in Great Britain by
Woolnough Bookbinding Ltd, Irthlingborough, Northamptonshire

CONDITIONS OF SALE
This book is sold subject to the condition that it shall not, by way of trade or otherwise, be lent,
re-sold, hired out or otherwise circulated without the publisher's prior consent in any form of
binding or cover other than that in which it is published and without a similar condition including
this condition being imposed on the subsequent purchaser.

All rights reserved. No part of this publication may be reproduced, stored in a retrieval system,
or transmitted, in any form or by any means, electronic, mechanical, photocopying, recording or
otherwise, without the prior permission of the publishers.

For Debbie,

'There are many good women, but you are the best!'

(PROVERBS 31:29)

HOW TO BRING OUT THE BEST FLAVOURS OF YOUR OWN PERSONAL 'BREAKFAST WITH GOD'

1 Order yourself a large cappuccino (with extra froth)

Personally, I find it really difficult to believe in God until I have had a cup of coffee in the morning.

2 Reflect and connect

The aim here is to learn about God and about you.

Let your mind connect with the themes and how you can add them to your life's experience.

Let your very soul reflect throughout the day on the various lessons learnt.

If you keep in mind what I have told you, the Lord will help you understand completely.

(2 Timothy 2:7)

3 Just do it! (Or if you are on a fast – just do without it!)

This book and your time will be a waste unless words get turned into works.

Faith that doesn't lead us to do good deeds is all alone and dead!

(James 2:17)

Dear God,
So far today, I've done all right.
I haven't gossiped, and I haven't lost my temper.
I haven't been grumpy, nasty or selfish.
But in a few minutes, God, I'm going to get out of bed
And that is when I'm going to need a lot of help.
Amen

(Found in the *Sunday Bulletin* of St Mary's Catholic Centre, Texas)

My hope is that this book helps you stay the course!

Duncan Banks, Banbury 2000

Orange Juice

When Jesus saw the crowds, he went up on the side of a mountain and sat down.

(MATTHEW 5:1)

CHOOSE THE VITAL

The Big Breakfast

Now hold on. Stop filming. Time out. This just can't be right. What on earth was Jesus doing, ignoring the crowd and wandering up a mountainside for a sit-down? Surely it was for the crowd that he came to earth in the first place? That crowd would have been full of sick people who needed healing and confused people who needed setting free. The crowd would have been bulging with lost people who needed saving. So what's with the hike up the hill?

I guess the answer is blatantly clear. In that moment Jesus saw what was pressing but chose what was a premium. In our own lives there will always be people and their demands crowding in, pressures and deadlines that scream at us. Unless we choose premium mountain-top moments with ourselves and our creator we will come to ruin. We need a daily dose of peace and perspective or we will burn out fast.

Phone calls, emails and diary deadlines will always demand our immediate response. Choosing to stand daily on the mountain top with God and breathing in the fresh air of his kingdom will give us new energy to face the madness of the market-place. If Jesus himself needed to schedule regular appointments with his Father ...

Continental

Bill Hybels is one of the world's most successful ministers. He is a spiritual advisor to Bill Clinton and leads Willow Creek Community Church, the largest church in America. Yet he confesses, 'If I do not set aside a time for a private meeting with God at least once every 24 hours, I tend to drift way off course spiritually.'

Coffee

Choose the vital right now. Choose to sit at the feet of Jesus. Choose a private meeting with God before the market-place comes crashing in today.

Orange Juice
The Heavens will disappear with a roar; the elements will be destroyed by fire and the earth will be laid bare. Since everything will be destroyed in this way, what kind of people ought you to be? *(2 PETER 3:10–11 NIV)*

THE SECRET PLACE REVEALED

The Big Breakfast
Read the verse above and imagine you are sitting in the soft seats of a multiplex cinema, eating popcorn and listening to a Hollywood-epic voice previewing the latest sci-fi blockbuster. It could well be a trailer to a modern-day movie, but the question that Peter asks in his 2,000-year-old letter is bang up to date: 'What kind of people ought we to be?' It's one we would do well to try to answer in this new millennium. Peter's next few words give us a good answer to be going on with.

You ought to be people of good and holy character …

Do you get his drift? If the world is going to come to an end and our lives fade away quicker than we imagine, let's invest now in the really important things of life. Not so much in our outward appearance, but on what our characters are like. The question being asked is, 'Who are you really, when no one else is looking?'

I guess we all have a clever public image carefully fashioned. We know who we are with others around us. The more painful and probing question is, 'What goes on under the surface and behind closed doors?' Answer that and you get a pretty good idea of how your God relationship is going.

Continental
I once stood in a packed tube train in London overhearing a conversation between two businessmen. One was attempting to describe a great new office colleague to the other. He quickly ran out of adjectives and said, 'I can only say, she has a beautiful soul.'

Coffee
I desperately want my soul life to be far more memorable than my public life. Take some time to consider your progress on your inner journey.

Orange Juice

No discipline seems pleasant at the time but painful. Later on, however, it produces a harvest … for those who have been trained by it.

(HEBREWS 12:11)

TRAINING THAT WORKS

The Big Breakfast

For the past few summers, I have travelled to Atlanta, Georgia, with a Christians in Sport team. We take a group of professional footballers each year to lead a soccer camp. Being a big footy fan, I love the chance to get to know the players and to play football with them. On my first visit I was stunned to be asked to play on the team. I even managed to convince an ex-QPR and Wolves soccer player to lend me his boots for the game. I laced them up, convinced that with these boots on my feet I would soon be playing for England. The truth was, I was terrible. Wearing the boots made no difference whatsoever.

I learnt the lesson. The reason my footballing buddy plays at the highest level is because he has disciplined himself to train hard every day, to work out in the gym, to eat the right food and get the right amount of rest. The disciplined life has turned him into a top sportsman. For me to wear his boots and expect to play like him was pure comic-book fantasy.

When it comes to the word 'discipline', I think we get the wrong idea. It conjures up images of school teachers or angry parents. If we are ever to achieve our dreams in life – dreams to be a success, to be a better friend, a better partner, even dreams to live as the Christian we have become – it will mean making discipline a close friend.

Continental

Proverbs gives this sound advice: 'All who refuse correction will be poor and disgraced' (Proverbs 13:18). It must be worth taking this seriously. To choose not to must be to choose ruin.

Coffee

Make a mental list of at least one place in your life where you need to begin to apply some discipline. The list may include food, leisure, entertainment, time …

Orange Juice
You know that many runners enter a race, and only one of them wins the prize. So run to win!

(1 CORINTHIANS 9:24)

FINISHING STRONG

The Big Breakfast
I went Grand Prix go-karting recently at a circuit not too far away. At the end of a dangerous day's driving, I ended up a dismal eleventh out of 40 other drivers. I still felt like Damon Hill as I sped bravely around the circuit at a top speed of 60 m.p.h. On the way home I realized that real Formula 1 cars reach speeds of 200 m.p.h. I suddenly felt less brave.

One of the greatest drivers of all time was Ayrton Senna who once drove a remarkable race, taking the chequered flag after starting sixteenth on the grid. No one rated his chances of getting on the winner's podium – no one, that is, except Senna himself.

You see, it's not really how you start the race that counts. It's all about finishing. Maybe you've started the race of life well, speeding down the back straight at 200 m.p.h. Or maybe you spun off into the 'kitty litter' at the first bend. The question is, will you be there at the chequered flag?

Now is the time to invest in the kind of things that will ensure we'll be there for the long haul.

Earning more money and buying more things won't guarantee we finish this race well. Maybe it's time to buy into some life skills such as peace-making or self-control.

Continental
Are the chicanes and constant pit stops of life wearing you out at the moment? Remember this: 'Our bodies are gradually dying, but we ourselves are being made stronger every day. These little troubles are getting us ready for an eternal glory that will make all our troubles seem like nothing' (2 Corinthians 4:16–17).

Coffee
The author Rudyard Kipling wrote, 'If you can fill the unforgiving minute/with sixty seconds' worth of distance run/yours is the Earth and everything that's in it. /And – what is more – you'll be a man, my son!'

Orange Juice

Just as iron sharpens iron, friends sharpen the minds of each other.

(PROVERBS 27:17)

LET THE SPARKS FLY

The Big Breakfast

Do you ever feel powerless to chop your way through the jungle of life? Sometimes I feel so blunt when it comes to standing strong in the face of deep temptation. I can so often feel I've lost my cutting edge when it comes to resolving those damaged relationships. So how do I get sharp again? Spend more time praying? Read a few more chapters of my 'Every-Other-Day with-Jesus' daily devotional? Put on a Delirious CD? All good stuff, but the Bible is clear on the best way to sharpen up. Read the verse again. We need to involve other people.

Of course, sparks fly when two bits of metal clash with each other. It's not an easy experience, but it's the only way to beat being blunt. Answer honestly. Who is passionately committed to your growth and development? When did you allow someone else you trust to open the door of your life and take a wander through?

The Salvation Army evangelist Phil Wall once said, 'Fewer might fall to the arch-enemy of Christian believers – money, sex and power – if only they had protected themselves with the honesty and accountability that any good relationship demands.'

Continental

The Beatles were so right when they sang, 'I get by with a little help from my friends.' We need to pursue sharpening relationships. The author Virginia Woolf made this profound statement: 'I have lost friends, some by death … others through a sheer inability to cross the street.' Make the effort!

Coffee

I love the wisdom of Proverbs. It is said of Billy Graham that he lives in the Proverbs. I once heard a preacher say that there are 31 chapters in Proverbs and 31 days in most months. It would do the soul good to read a chapter a day.

Orange Juice

But if we confess our sins to God, he can always be trusted to forgive us and take our sins away.

(1 JOHN 1:9)

NOT GUILTY!

The Big Breakfast

Have you ever woken up on a winter's morning and seen the pure white snow transform your grubby neighbourhood? Have you ever played in goal and felt the joy of keeping a clean sheet despite letting in six in the last game? Have you ever felt your whole body sigh with relief as you take your heavy rucksack off after a long hike? Have you ever known the indescribable joy of hearing your Father in heaven declare you 'not guilty' as you confess your failure to him?

Sin and guilt are responsible for crippling both Christian and unbeliever alike. The head of one of London's largest psychiatric institutes said, 'I could release half of my patients today if only they could be assured of forgiveness.' So how do we get rid of sin?

Sin leaves the body through the mouth. John says that 'If we *confess* our sins' then God will rush in with wave after wave of purifying snow. If we open our mouths and tell him how sorry we are then we can know a clean sheet between heaven and us. If we let the words of wrongdoing out of our mouths then the rucksack of past failure can be abandoned at the foot of the cross and we can stand tall once again.

Why do we hang on to our sin like some security blanket when the freedom of forgiveness is just a confession away?

Continental

I have made it my aim to begin reducing the gap between the time I mess up and the time I say sorry, until one day the gap will get so small I can almost catch myself before I fall. Remember that God is never shocked with us. We shouldn't put off our confession to him out of embarrassment.

Coffee

If you let unconfessed sin pile up, it will only drive a wedge between God and your soul. Open your mouth and get it straightened out right now.

Orange Juice
Love the LORD your God with all your heart, soul, and mind.

(MATTHEW 22:37)

EMBRACE THE EMOTION

The Big Breakfast
So, Jesus says that the command is to 'love God with all your heart'. The heart is the centre of our emotion. Ever heard a sports coach shout, 'Put your heart into it!' or a ditched lover say, 'She broke my heart!'? In the Old Testament, it wasn't the heart but the bowels the writers used to describe our emotional centre. It's a good job Graham Kendrick wasn't writing songs back then.

Jesus is saying that the kind of relationship he wants with his followers is an emotional one. Trouble is, for many of us the emotional side of our lives has been sucked dry. For me, being British meant that I had to keep my upper lip stiff in all circumstances. I was always told as a kid that 'big boys don't cry', and then on my first trip to church I was told to keep my emotions separate from my faith and my worship.

I guess my wife could prove her love for me by constantly showing me a copy of our marriage certificate. However, I for one am much keener to discover the emotional side of our relationship. I would swap a bit of paper for a passionate kiss any day! Loving God with all our heart means loving with all heartfelt passion and romance. Only then do we move on to our souls and our minds.

Continental
Someone once asked this question: 'Why is it that if a film produces laughter it's regarded as successful, or if a football match thrills the spectators it's reviewed as exciting, but if the congregation are moved by the glory of God in worship it's excused as emotionalism?'

Coffee
It's said that 'experience is not what happens to someone; it's what someone does with what happens to them'. So what will you do with that experience of holy, heartfelt emotion?

Orange Juice

God blesses those people who refuse evil advice ... Instead, the Law of the LORD makes them happy, and they think about it day and night.

(PSALM 1:1-2)

THE BIG MAC BIBLE

The Big Breakfast

One of the McDonald's in my town has a 'drive-through' window. From the comfort of the driver's seat you can order a Big Mac, fries and a drink — it only takes an instant. And it doesn't take much longer to consume it in the car park.

In Paris there is a restaurant called La Parisian where I once had a meal with some friends. We spent four hours enjoying the cuisine and the company — course after course of delicious delicacies.

Why is it that we so often reduce the essential food of the faith to a Big Mac meal that only ever gives us a dose of spiritual indigestion? How do we turn the 'Law of the Lord' into our delight? How can it become as appetizing as a fine French meal?

The answer must be to do all we can to dust off the Bible on the bookshelf and make it our manual for life. We must do all we can to discipline our diary to digest it — after all, we always seem to find time for food, our friends and even our favourite TV shows. We must create an inspirational environment in which to read it, write a journal to help apply it, and find a suitable translation to understand it.

Continental

The Psalmist goes on to tell of the results of making God's Word a delight in our daily lives. We will become like a tree that yields fruit (character growth) and a leaf that doesn't wither (perseverance), and whatever we do will prosper. Good, eh?

Coffee

So what translation of the Bible do you read? Take C.S. Lewis's advice: 'A modern translation is for the most purposes far more useful than the Authorised version.' Try the CEV — it works for me.

Orange Juice

Jesus went up a mountainside and called to him those he wanted, and they came to him. He appointed twelve … *that they might be with him* and that he might send them out to preach.

(MARK 3:13-14)

MORE THAN A TV SHOW?

The Big Breakfast

Jesus' first reason for calling twelve followers was 'that they might be with him'. If the Son of God needed people around him, then how much more do we need key relationships feeding into our lives?

Over the years I have discovered that the kind of friend we are dictates the kind of friends we attract. If we are not finding those 'soul mate' kinds of friendships, then maybe we need to take a long hard look in the mirror.

We must develop a close network of relationships if we are ever to stand strong in the tough times of life and create memories in the good. I love my Silverstone moments with Dave, and my Stratford moments with Leon.* (I love laughing with Chris, Sheena and Caroline. I love travelling everywhere I go at the moment with Dan. I love summer days with Alastair and Debbie. Then of course there's Rob, Andy, Nigel, Pete and Gerard, Dawn, Ben, Joel and Steve … the list goes on. The names mean nothing to you but everything to me. They have taken a lifetime to find and will take a lifetime to keep.

* Silverstone is the British Formula 1 racing circuit, and Stratford, of course, is Shakespeare's birthplace!

Continental

Back in the 1980s, the world watched as nine paraplegic Olympians lined up for the 100 metres, each with a passion to win. The race began and one runner, out in front, tripped and fell. He expected to see his competitors leave him behind, but they all stopped, picked him up and ran over the finish line together. Who picks you up when you fall?

Coffee

Philip Zimbardo, a world authority on psychology at Stanford University, said: 'I know of no more potent killer than isolation. There is no more destructive influence on physical and mental health than the isolation of you from me.' Get together with a friend today.

Orange Juice

That evening the disciples came to Jesus and said, 'This place is like a desert, and it is already late. Let the crowds leave, so they can ... buy some food.' Jesus replied, *'They don't have to leave. Why don't you give them something to eat?'*

(MATTHEW 14:14–16)

GIVE UP YOUR LUNCH BOX

The Big Breakfast

If only the Church could grab this one, we would really begin to live as God intended and the world would sit up and take note.

The crowd was large and the hour late. The disciples felt it their duty to let Jesus know that they had heard one or two rumbling tummies, with their own sounding the loudest. The nearest burger joint was quite a distance away.

The Master's answer showed them, as it shows us, who is responsible for feeding the hungry. It's not primarily governments or aid agencies. 'They don't have to leave. Why don't you give them something to eat?'

It is your responsibility to feed the hungry in our world. I know you don't have enough to solve the problem. Neither did the disciples.

'We have only five small loaves of bread and two fish.' Jesus didn't need them to have enough – they just had to be willing to give what they had. What can you give today to the man on the street or the project in your town? The axiom is true: if you're not part of the solution, you're part of the problem.

Continental

When the disciples gave of their little, the Master gave of his abundance. He turned a packed lunch into a feast for thousands of hungry people. The miracle went so 'above and beyond' that they collected 12 basketloads of leftovers. A friend of mine suggested that would make one for every disciple to take home!

Coffee

The great wartime British prime minister Winston Churchill said, 'The price of greatness is responsibility.' Aspire to greatness, and make feeding the hungry your responsibility.

Orange Juice

Delight yourself in the LORD and he will give you the desires of your heart.

(PSALM 37:4 NIV)

THE DISCIPLINE OF DELIGHT

The Big Breakfast

I'm sure you've got a whole stack of excellent desires for your life. Some very laudable ones even – desires to find the right person to marry, to find the right career to do, even desires to serve God in some shape or form. We must never let these desires fade as age grows, lest we give in to mediocrity.

However, the flip side of having a heartfelt desire or vision is invariably frustration and disappointment. I read recently of one lucky tourist who inadvertently won 2 million francs for being the two millionth visitor to the Eiffel Tower. How must the person behind him in the queue have felt? Total disappointment, no doubt.

Maybe today you are disappointed with God because he just doesn't seem to make a difference. You've failed an exam that you worked and prayed so hard about, you didn't get that promotion, a special relationship has failed, you prayed for the sick on Sunday and they got a whole lot worse.

Truth is, you can't talk about being a Christian without talking about disappointment. Maybe the key is to put those good desires to one side for a period and get back to where that verse from Psalms starts: 'Delight yourself in the LORD.' Maybe … just maybe, God will pick those desires up and make them his desires for you.

Continental

The evangelist Smith Wigglesworth once said, 'Great faith is a product of great fights. Great testimonies are an outcome of great tests. Great triumphs can only come after great trials.' The reality is that the victory crown Jesus wore was a crown of thorns.

Coffee

The Bible says 'don't be afraid' 366 times. That's one for every day of the year – even in a leap year! What a great place to start this new discipline of delight.

Orange Juice

If I live, it will be for Christ, and if I die, I will gain even more… I could keep on living and doing something useful. It is a hard choice to make. I want to die and be with Christ, because that would be much better.

(PHILIPPIANS 1:21–3)

TORN

The Big Breakfast

How can Paul talk like that? Has he no fear of death? I guess not. For me, I would choose to be alive on planet earth every time. I once saw a little ditty about a gravestone eulogy that said:

Remember, friend, when passing by,
As you are now so once was I.
As I am now soon you will be.
Prepare for death and follow me.

Someone etched this along the bottom:

To follow you I'm not content
Until I know which way you went!

The truth is that, as believers, we know where we are going. That's why we don't need to fear death. The great preacher D.L. Moody said, 'Someday you will read in the papers that Moody is dead. Don't believe a word of it. At that moment I shall be more alive than I am now … I was born in the flesh in 1837; I was born of the Spirit in 1855. That which is born of the flesh may die. That which is born of the Spirit shall live for ever.'

Continental

'What God has planned for people who love him is more than eyes have seen or ears have heard. It has never even entered our minds!' (1 Corinthians 2:9). If you were to give Steven Spielberg the brief to make a movie about heaven, then even his brilliantly creative mind could never begin to conceive the presentation God has ready to roll.

Coffee

I remember reading *Peter Pan* as a kid and being filled with hope when he says to his chums, 'To die will be an awfully big adventure.' You don't need to be afraid.

Orange Juice

Jesus came walking on the water towards his disciples … They were terrified …
Jesus said to them, 'Don't worry! I am Jesus. Don't be afraid.' Peter replied,
'Lord, if it is really you, tell me to come to you on the water.'

(MATTHEW 14:25-8)

CARPE DIEM

The Big Breakfast

My favourite film of all time is *Dead Poets Society.*
You must get it out on video – it's pure
inspiration for the soul. At the start of the film
the new teacher, Mr Keating (played by Robin Williams), takes
his new class into the great hall to view the trophies and old
sepia pictures of Helton boys from an age past. 'They are now
food for worms, boys,' Keating tells the class. 'Listen closely as
they whisper their legacy to you.' As the boys lean in towards
the glass cabinets, the teacher whispers these haunting words
on their behalf: '*Carpe diem*. Seize the day. Make your lives
extraordinary.' As an old man, I don't want to look back on my
life with nothing but regrets. I want to be a person who made
life extraordinary. Who took risks once in a while.

Preachers are so good at knocking Peter for his lack of
faith. I have heard them say, 'If only he had kept his eyes on
Jesus he would never have sunk.' The truth is, he is the only
person on planet earth, besides Jesus, who has ever walked
on water. At least he got out of the boat while the rest
missed out on making their lives extraordinary. 'Peter then got
out of the boat and started walking on the water towards
him' (Matthew 14:29).

Continental

A good friend of
mine once had the
incredible privilege of
interviewing Billy
Graham in New York.
He asked him for
some words of
wisdom from an
older man to a
younger. Billy Graham
responded by simply
saying, 'I never knew
it would go so
quickly. I still feel
eighteen years old.
Just don't waste a
moment of it.' Where
will the adventure of
faith begin for you
today?

Coffee

Don't you think that the idea of having to die without having lived is
unbearable?

Orange Juice
Do not wear yourself out to get rich; have the wisdom to show restraint.

(PROVERBS 23:4 NIV)

THE ANTIDOTE

The Big Breakfast
This is going to hurt, but 'wounds from a friend' and all that … Let me tell you a tough truth. Materialism is the biggest challenge to this generation. We've got sucked in bad. The advertisers have convinced us that luxuries are necessities and that we just can't do without them. They have filled our lives with so much stuff that our priorities have drifted off course. It is getting almost impossible to keep up unless you have an endless supply of time and money.

The only antidote to spiralling materialism is giving, and giving extravagantly. Trouble is, our generation is renowned as being the poorest givers ever. Lasting contentment doesn't come from getting more things. John D. Rockefeller was asked how much money a person needs to be truly happy. 'Just a little bit more!' he said. Being satisfied means having fewer wants, not 'wearing ourselves out to get rich'.

A friend of mine managed to break the cycle of buying clothes she didn't really need by holding a twelve-month clothes fast. She saved a heap of wardrobe space and a stack of cash. She got a bigger buzz than shopping by giving a lot of it away to the poor. It sometimes takes drastic measures to get our eyes fixed on Jesus again (Hebrews 12:2).

Continental
' "A few seeds make a small harvest, but a lot of seeds make a big harvest." Each of you must make up your own mind about how much to give. But don't feel sorry that you must give … God loves people who love to give.' Paul's advice to the Corinthian church (2 Corinthians 9:6–7) is as valid now as it was then. What have you cheerfully decided to give this week?

Coffee
Consider this: 'Don't wear yourself out trying to get rich; restrain yourself! Riches disappear in the blink of an eye; wealth sprouts wings and flies off into the wild blue yonder' (*The Message*).

Orange Juice

Come to my home each day and listen to me. You will find happiness. By finding me, you find life.

(PROVERBS 8:34–5)

THE LOST ART OF REFLECTION

The Big Breakfast

Reflection – the art of waiting on God – is the lost art of the twenty-first century. A business friend of mine told me how he used to rush out of the house every morning, drive bumper to bumper and arrive at the office just on time. His daily routine sounded frantic. Then one fine summer's day he had a late morning meeting and therefore didn't have quite the same manic rush. He left later, eased off on the accelerator and lifted his head a little. Despite having made the same daily journey for years, he noticed trees and wildlife he had never seen before. He even pulled the car off the road and took time to stop, and breathe the fresh air. He thought of his life, his work, his family and his faith. He discovered a moment of quiet reflection that has revolutionized his life. Now it has become a regular practice. Pull over for a moment and let me ask you some questions that will lead you into the wonder of personal reflection.

How is your walk with God today? What books are stimulating your thinking? How are things going with your partner? How are your energy levels? Are you pleased with your physical fitness? Is sexual temptation getting the better of you? When did you last do something just for fun? If Satan was to trip you, how would he do it? Do you like yourself?

Continental

A. W. Tozer writes in *The Pursuit of God*, 'It is important that we get still to wait on God. And it is best that we get alone, preferably with our Bible outstretched before us. Then we will draw near to God and begin to hear him speak to us in our hearts.'

Coffee

'Blessed is the man, blessed is the woman, who listens to me, awake and ready each morning … as I start my day's work' (Proverbs 8:34–5 *The Message*).

Orange Juice

Peter and the other two disciples had been sound asleep. All at once they woke up and saw how glorious Jesus was.

LUKE 9:32

WAKE UP!

The Big Breakfast

What I wouldn't give to see the glory of God right before my eyes. You tell me anything that could beat that.

My good friend Ian is a big Formula 1 motor racing fan. He had watched every race in the season and like millions of others stayed up to the early hours to watch Damon Hill win the 1996 world championship in Japan. He kept awake until the warm-up lap at 3 a.m. Then he closed his eyes for what he thought was just a blink – and opened them again to the chimes of Big Ben ushering in the six o'clock morning news. He had missed out on one of the most memorable races of the decade.

Jesus had taken his closest friends, Peter, James and John, up a mountainside to pray. The Master gets down on his knees, while the disciples curl up under the stars for a doze and nearly miss out on the fireworks as heaven touches earth. 'While he was praying, his face changed, and his clothes became shining white' (Luke 9:29). Imagine missing out on that.

So where do you feel dozy in your spiritual life? Once the passion burnt like a bolt from heaven. Nothing would stop you making your life dreams come true. Now, your passion lies dormant, fast asleep, waiting for a spark to set the fire burning again.

Continental

The British Chief Rabbi Jonathan Sacks once said, 'Death is more universal than life. Everybody dies but not everybody lives.' Wake up before you fall asleep for good!

Coffee

Wake up! Don't sleep through the race of life and miss out on seeing the glory of God.

Orange Juice

I have put roads in deserts, streams in thirsty lands.

(ISAIAH 43:19)

The Big Breakfast

I love this apocryphal story about two camels conversing. One sunny day, little Baby Camel asked big Mummy Camel why camels have such big feet, such long eyelashes and such huge humps. 'Well, darling,' said Mum wisely, 'when we are in the desert we need big feet to walk over the shifting sand. We need long eyelashes to protect our eyes from sandstorms, and big humps to carry water on long journeys.'

'So, Mummy,' replied the baby camel, 'why are we in London Zoo?'

Good question. You see camels were designed to live in the deserts, not in concrete cages. You and I have a faith that is designed to work best in the deserts and wastelands of our world. Not cooped up in the cage of Church. Maybe that's why it goes stale so often.

Where are the wastelands of your world? Is it the local council estate, the shopping centre, the retirement homes, the heath clinic? The list is endless. Unless we are prepared to journey to these places, often places where we feel like we don't belong, we will never uncage the gospel and let it loose on a broken world.

Continental

Martin Luther King Jr once said, 'A man has not started living until he can rise above the narrow confines of his own existence to the broader concerns of others.' Is it time to take your eyes off yourself and start looking to the needs of others?

Coffee

A note was passed around a crowd as they gathered in the capital prior to a revolution to overthrow an evil dictator. It read simply: 'If not now, when? If not us, who?'

Orange Juice

You are the salt of the earth, but if the salt loses its saltiness, how can it be made salty again? … You are the light of the world … Let your light shine before men, that they may see your good deeds and praise your Father in heaven.

(MATTHEW 5:13–16)

STOP THE ROT

The Big Breakfast

A friend of mine was asked to pick up an African evangelist from Heathrow Airport and transport him to various venues around the country to preach. He said he had never met such a fearless evangelist. One time, they stopped for lunch at a roadside café and my friend's African guest stood to his feet, quietened the crowd of customers and gave a short gospel message. He even got a rousing round of applause!

I just could never do that. Does that make me a failure in sharing my faith? Absolutely not. Jesus never said, 'Go and be salt' or 'You must be a light in a dark world.' He said, 'You *are* salt' and 'You *are* light.' In other words, you will not be able to help yourself being the preserving salt as you live in a society where values continue to rot away. You can't help lighting up the right path for a generation that stumbles around in the darkness. Doesn't that take the guilt of failed evangelistic attempts away? You see, some are called to preach to stadiums full of people and others to roadside cafés, whereas most are called to rush headlong into our world, enjoy what is good and allow the taste and brightness of our God-filled lives to change what is bad.

Continental

The eminent theologian John Stott once said, 'It is time for Christians to stop blaming the meat of society for going rotten when the preserving salt has been taken out.'

Coffee

St Francis of Assisi had a similar thought when he told his followers to 'Preach the gospel at all times and if necessary, use words.'

Orange Juice

Now go, but remember: I am sending you like lambs into a pack of wolves.

(LUKE 10:3)

UNCAGE THE BUNNY

The Big Breakfast

The biggest mistake I made in my marriage was allowing Debbie to convince me to buy a rabbit. She said we were just going to 'pop in for a look' and I ended up walking out with a cute, lop-eared baby bunny that we named Dylan. However, after a couple of years (and the birth of our first son) Dylan started to get neglected. I thought about letting him go in a field near our house, but the vet said Dylan would be dead within a day: 'He is a tamed rabbit. He can no longer survive outside his cage.'

I think that is exactly what the Church has done with young people. We've sold you a taming faith that means you can no longer survive in the habitat you were created for. We've told you to get converted from your sin but haven't helped you in getting fully converted to the purposes of God. That purpose is not simply to survive in a cage called Church but to thrive in the place we call the real world.

As a church leader, I want to say sorry and to ask you to leave a different legacy to the next generation. Prepare them to live like lambs in a pack of wolves.

Continental

Business guru Charles Handy is one of my favourite authors. He asks this question in *The Age of Paradox*: if we didn't exist, would we recreate ourselves and what would this new creation look like? Ask this of your church community.

Coffee

Martin Luther King Jr once said, 'This generation will not be judged for the evil bad people have done but for the appalling silence of the good.' Shout this forgotten message out loud to a new generation.

Orange Juice

We announce the message about Christ, and we use all our wisdom to warn and teach everyone, so that all Christ's followers will grow and become *mature*.

(COLOSSIANS 1:28)

CHARACTER OR COMPETENCE?

The Big Breakfast

Gulf War Commander Stormin' Norman Schwartzkopf said, 'Character is the fundamental attribute of all great leaders. Competence is important, certainly, but if I had to sacrifice one I would give up competence before character. Character is everything.' It's our characters that measure our maturity in Christ, not our competence.

As a leader, it recently dawned on me that it probably wouldn't be my abilities that let me down, but my character. Yet I spend far more time sharpening my gifts than my character. It was never Bill Clinton's ability as orator or statesman that let him down, but his character. I doubt anyone will say, 'Duncan, you're getting boring and we don't want you to preach any more, so push off.' If I fell, I'm sure it would be because of a character failure.

As a young evangelist, I was given great opportunity to develop my gifts, but no one ever worked with me on the secret life issues. I soon came crashing down. When the tough times came (and they always do), my ability to tell a few stories didn't keep me strong. Only strength of character does that. Where are you investing your development time?

Continental

Best-selling business writer Steven Covey talks about a huge paradigm shift in business leadership development. He says, 'Over the past 50 years leadership development has mainly focused on the development of skills in management. In the future, leadership development will focus on developing people of character, depth and integrity.'

Coffee

It's been said that the true test of character is not how much we know how to do, but how we behave when we don't know what to do.

Orange Juice

But the fruit of the spirit is love, joy, peace, patience, kindness, goodness, faithfulness, gentleness and self-control. Against such things there is no law.

(GALATIANS 5:22 NIV)

GET FRUITY

The Big Breakfast

I became a Christian in my mid-teens. I had been putting it off for ages because I had a fear that when I got saved I would have to become like some of the people in church. I didn't suit white socks and sandals, and tank tops were definitely not my style! I was not into Cliff and didn't want to sing in the choir. My understanding of what a Christian looked like was a total misunderstanding. The best description that I've found is the fruit list above – that's what a real believer looks like.

So how can we tell if the spiritual fruit in our lives is growing well? Ask yourself this question: when life bumps into you, what spills out?

I have many heroes in the faith, some dead, some very much alive. One such person brimming with life is an older and wiser man called Joel. I spent four weeks travelling the country with him, watching him and learning from him. He has a very responsible job and when life bumped into him (and boy, did it come crashing in at times) do you know what always spilt out? You got it, love, joy, peace …

See what comes tumbling out of you today as life comes tumbling in.

Continental

How many fruit can you count? No, this is not *Sesame Street*. I want to make a point. Paul says 'fruit' (singular) not 'fruits' (plural). In the supermarket you can choose to put some fruit in your basket and leave others on the shelf. In God's economy, he wants to develop our whole character.

Coffee

Reread this character list of Paul's. Identify where you feel weak. Make a deliberate choice to take it off the shelf today and ask God to help you work on it.

Orange Juice

Remove the chains of prisoners who are chained unjustly. Free those who are abused! Share your food with everyone who is hungry; share your home with the poor and homeless ... Then your light will shine like the dawning sun.

(ISAIAH 58:6–8)

REVIVAL GUARANTEED

The Big Breakfast

What a great description of revival! How I long for the day when the light of the gospel rises in the darkness of this godless age and the dim witness of the Church becomes as brilliant as the sunshine in the middle of the day. I want to see that day in this nation before I die.

So how do we get there? More fervent prayer meetings? Wouldn't do any harm. More electric worship services? Sounds appealing. More seeker-sensitive presentations? We need them, too.

Hang on. Read the Isaiah verse again, and the answer shines through clearly: the good stuff from heaven comes down when we start spending ourselves on behalf of the hungry and satisfying the needs of the oppressed. One translation suggests we 'lavish on the poor the same affection we lavish on ourselves'.

The truth is, some often look over the sea to other revivals but wouldn't dream of looking over our street to the lonely pensioner or stressed single mum.

Continental

I know there is a God-given passion in you to be part of a revival generation, and I think I know how you can get there. Hunt out those in need, the hungry and the voiceless, the poor and the disenfranchised. Spend yourself on them and satisfy their needs. Then your light will shine ...

Coffee

'The wicked don't care about the rights of the poor, but good people do' (Proverbs 29:7). Which are you – good or wicked?

Orange Juice

Large crowds were travelling with Jesus, and turning to them he said: 'If anyone comes to me and does not hate his father and mother, his wife and children, his brothers and sisters – yes, even his own life – he cannot be my disciple.'

(LUKE 14:26 NIV)

HATE YOUR MUM AND DAD

The Big Breakfast

At first reading, I guess that just about counts me out as a disciple. I love my folks, my wife and my kids. I don't hate them. And doesn't the Bible say somewhere we should honour our parents and love our wives and not exasperate our children? What was Jesus getting at here?

The answer is at the start of the verse. Jesus wasn't into hangers-on. He was every marketing man's nightmare, with no interest in big numbers. He wanted to whittle down a large crowd of sightseers. He wanted people who were committed.

I don't believe for one moment that he meant us to treat our closest family with hate. In trying to lose the uncommitted from the crowd, he suggests that his followers must have no higher priority in life than loving him. Debbie is my life and my everything. I am devoted to my two boys and would travel to the ends of the earth for them. Mum and Dad are my two greatest heroes. Yet my devotion to Jesus must always come before them. Tough one, isn't it?

Continental

How do your close personal relationships line up against the Master? Can you honestly say that in a competition he would come first every time? Is Jesus really the number one relationship you have? If not, *you cannot be his disciple.*

Coffee

'My son, give up self and you will find me. Lose the right to choose and the right to own, and you will know nothing but gain. Abundant grace will be heaped upon you the moment you surrender your own will and do not claim it back' (Thomas à Kempis).

Orange Juice

You cannot be my disciple unless you carry your own cross and come with me.

(LUKE 14:27)

DYING TO LIVE

The Big Breakfast

We're still on the subject of being committed Christ followers. Jesus shaves some more onlookers off the large crowd following him with another outrageous statement. Carrying a cross in his day was a familiar picture of crucifixion and death. Was he really saying his followers had to take their own lives? Don't be daft. To 'come with Jesus' means to die to our way of life and live for his. It means sacrificing unhealthy ambition and to 'offer your bodies to him as a living sacrifice' (Romans 12:1).

A youth leader of mine from years back became the youngest elder our church had ever seen. The following week, his boss offered him a partnership in the business. It would mean a huge salary, a Jag and a big house in the country. It would also mean giving up all his time to the company. What should he do? He felt so called by God to serve the youth of our church, but the business offer was tempting. This verse from Luke convinced him that to 'be his disciple' he had to give up his own way for God's way. He said no to the boss and yes to the King. Following Christ means the highest level of commitment. We are not called to a Sunday-school picnic but to a bloody battleground.

Continental

The kind of radical devotion this verse demands is rare today. Maybe that's why, in Jesus' day, many of his disciples said, 'This is a difficult statement' when they heard it. As a result of it, many withdrew and were not walking with him any more (John 6:60, 66). Have you got what it takes to call yourself a disciple of Jesus today?

Coffee

John Wesley was asked what he would do if tomorrow were his last day on earth. His answer showed the contentment he had with his devotion to God – 'Nothing different.' Are you content with your walk as you reflect today?

Orange Juice

So then, you cannot be my disciple unless you give away everything you own.

(LUKE 14:33)

GIVE IT ALL AWAY

The Big Breakfast

This is a real toughie. I so wish Jesus had never said it. You see, I love my stuff. I can't image life without my Nintendo 64 or my CD player. And where would I be without my beautiful bottle of Issey Myake after-shave or my mobile phone with built-in daily planner? Maybe it's this attitude that so often waters down the intensity of my life with Christ.

This 'giving it all up' statement from Jesus must have lost loads from the crowd. It was designed to weed out the spectators from the participators. Get the perspective right, though. I don't think he means that we can't possess anything, but that we mustn't let things possess us. To be a real disciple means to hold stuff loosely.

What do you need to hold a little less tight? What comes between you and your maker? You see, I don't think that all believers automatically become disciples. It's one thing to believe, but it's another to believe enough to let go of relationships that get in the way, ambition that distracts and the stuff that shifts our priorities. The author and pastor Philip Yancey said, 'The poor, not the rich, have perseverance for life. Why? Because they have nothing else to hang on to.'

Continental

So which one of the words in this verse don't you understand? It's blatantly clear, isn't it? Let go of 'things' and grab on to God. In *The Pursuit of God*, A.W. Tozer said, 'There is no doubt that this possessive clinging to things is one of the most harmful habits of life. Because it is so natural it is rarely recognized for the evil that it is.'

Coffee

Rudyard Kipling remarked, in an address to university students, 'As you go through life, don't seek for fame, or money, or for power, because one day you will meet a man who cares for none of these things, and then you will realize how poor you are.'

Orange Juice
But you must stay calm and be willing to suffer. You must work hard to tell the good news and to do your job well.

(2 TIMOTHY 4:5)

DON'T QUIT

The Big Breakfast
Sound advice from Paul the apostle to his young apprentice, Timothy. He had been telling him how others were throwing the towel in but that he needed a bit of endurance.

Did you ever see the classic film *Chariots of Fire*? It's a great movie that charts the young Scottish missionary Eric Liddell as he trains for the Olympics. His sister tries to encourage him to hang up his running shoes and go to the Chinese mission field as his father and grandfather did. 'Aye, Jen,' he says, 'I know that God made me to be a missionary and that is what I will be. But he also made me fast, and when I run I feel his pleasure.'

You may not be a famous missionary or have a teacher like Paul. You may not fill stadiums with your preaching like Billy Graham or rewrite a nation's history like Martin Luther King Jr, but where do you feel the pleasure of God? Is it in the way you do your job or the way you have been able to share your faith? Do you feel God's pleasure as you serve others, expecting nothing in return? Even if nobody else says thanks, your endurance does not go unnoticed in heaven. Feel his pleasure today.

Continental
Winston Churchill was once asked to speak to the students at Oxford University. As you can image, the hall was packed as the great man extinguished his famous cigar and stood to the podium. His most memorable speech ever lasted just four words: 'Young people – don't quit!'

Coffee
I know you've thought of giving up, but don't – endure some more.

Orange Juice

The LORD your God … is always with you. He celebrates and sings because of you, and he will refresh your life with his love.

(ZEPHANIAH 3:17)

YOUR NAME IS THE TITLE TRACK

The Big Breakfast

I thought I'd better read Zephaniah's book just in case I bump into him in heaven. It could be so embarrassing otherwise. Actually, I'm glad I did. It has given me an insight into the character of God that I had never thought about before.

What a great picture of a God who 'celebrates and sings because of you'. He gets up in the morning (figuratively speaking, you understand), throws open the windows of heaven and sings about you. It's your name that he repeats in the chorus. It's your name that features in the refrain. In fact, it's your name that is the title track of the whole album God has written about you and which he plays for his pleasure.

If that thought doesn't 'refresh your life with his love', I don't know what will. If you can indulge me and allow your imagination to be stretched a little, you could almost picture a part of God's character like that of a doting grandfather. He has your picture on his mantelpiece and is always trying to twist the conversation with the angels around to talking about you. He's so proud of you.

So if you hear a heavenly song or some heavenly chatter this morning, it just might be about you.

Continental

The three most awesome words you will ever hear running through your brain and filtering down into the emotional centre of your heart are 'God loves you'. Let me say it again – 'God loves you'. He loves you enough never to leave you, even though you may walk away from him. His great delight is in you, right now, as you read this book.

Coffee

I love this line that my mate Mark wrote in a worship song: 'My Father, music from your lips puts the beat back into my heart and the joy back into my walk.' Rock on!

Orange Juice

Who may ascend the hill of the LORD? Who may stand in his holy place? He who has clean hands and a pure heart, who does not lift up his soul to an idol ... such is the generation of those who seek him.

(PSALM 24:3-6 NIV)

CLEAN HANDS, PURE HEART

The Big Breakfast

Have you ever had one of those 'penny-dropping' moments where the lights just seem to come on for the first time on the really obvious things of life? I had been speaking at a big youth festival and was well into my second week when the band Delirious arrived. It was a most memorable gig as five thousand of us squashed into a crowded cowshed to see them perform.

God grabbed my attention through one simple song introduction by Martin Smith, 'Who can get up to where God is? Who can stand in his holy place?' He left a pause. My heart leapt inside. That's where I wanted to be. He gave the answer. 'Only those of us with clean hands and pure hearts.'

That's it! That's why I so often feel in the valley rather than on the mountain top. My hands are dirty. The things I get my hands into are often not pleasing to God. My heart is not clean. I haven't guarded my heart well. I have allowed my eyes to watch, my ears to hear and my mouth to talk about stuff that is just not pure. No wonder I rarely walk up the holy mountain to where my God is.

Continental

The two hallmarks of a God-seeking generation are purity of action and holiness of character. If your eyes are the windows to your heart, what stuff should you be averting your gaze from today? If your hands are the tools of your service, what things should you be letting go of?

Coffee

'You'll do best by filling your minds and meditating on things true, noble, reputable, authentic, compelling, gracious – the best, not worst; the beautiful, not the ugly; things to praise not things to curse' (Philippians 4:8 *The Message*).

Orange Juice
Respect your father and your mother, and you will live a long time in the land I am giving you.

(EXODUS 20:12)

BRINGING UP YOUR PARENTS

The Big Breakfast
Mark Twain once said something like, 'When I was fourteen my father was so stupid I could hardly bear him. But by the time I was twenty-one I was so amazed at how much he had learned in seven years.' Often it's only in hindsight that we can give our folks the honour and respect for the influence they have had on our lives. While they are far from perfect, they deserve our gratitude. I love my mum and dad dearly, but I was thirty years old before I really told them how grateful I am for them. I wrote them a letter trying to express it. The reply from my dad is a treasured memory that I carry with me wherever I go. Here's an extract: 'Well son, what a wonderful letter to receive, reading it certainly brought tears to our eyes … I must say we have often wondered what you thought of us as parents … I think back to those summer holidays, we did have some fun didn't we, but then I always had fun with you.'

What have you always wanted to say to honour your folks? Say it soon, before it's too late.

Continental
The fifth commandment is the only one with a promise attached. If we treat our parents with honour and respect we will live a long life. Find a way today to be creative in your affection for your folks.

Coffee
Billy Graham once said that 'nobody ever said on their death bed that they wished they'd spent more time at the office'. If you still can, plan this week to change your schedule and pick up the phone, write or even call round to see your parents.

Orange Juice
Anyone who belongs to Christ Jesus and wants to live right will have trouble from others.

(2 TIMOTHY 3:12)

THE GENUINE ARTICLE

The Big Breakfast
Sometimes the best encouragement to one's soul is to hear it how it truly is. So here goes: the truth is if you love Jesus you will be persecuted. If 'to live right' is your pursuit then pain along the path is a certainty. For some it's no more than a loss of pride, but for others it can mean the loss of life.

The true story is told of a priest in communist Russia who one Sabbath was leading the service of the weary faithful when the ancient building began to echo with the sound of kalashnikov rifles loading up. The meeting had been disturbed by a group of militiamen and their angry-sounding leader. He told the crowd that any Christian left in the building would be shot in two minutes. Some hurried out. Others remained, holding firm to what they believed. Eventually the militia leader told the trembling few that he wasn't going to shoot anyone today; he needed to hear about Jesus and he wanted to make sure he heard it from the 'genuine article'.

Persecution at any level will serve as a good test to our commitment. Be honest, are you really the 'genuine article' to the people closest to you?

Continental
I think the most painful persecution comes from your own kind. Why does the Army of Christ enjoy shooting itself in the foot, stabbing itself in the back and tearing itself apart in civil war? Don't provoke persecution, but expect it. Don't fight each other, but support each other in life's daily battles.

Coffee
One of the few Greek words I know is *martorea* – the Greek word for witness. You will know something of the pain of being a 'martyr' as you witness to a broken world, but you're in great company.

Orange Juice

I will build my church, and death itself will not have any power over it.

(MATTHEW 16:18)

GOD'S THEATRE ON EARTH

The Big Breakfast

It's that same gritty determination of Jesus that seemed to rub off on the early Church. It's almost as if you need some 'attitude' to follow Christ. There is a sense in which God loves angry young people. Take the big boys of the Bible. What have Moses, David and Paul got in common? Well, for one, they were all murderers. Moses killed a man, David slept with another man's wife, then bumped him off to cover his tracks, and Paul was a serial killer. Yet God took their passions and shaped them for good, not bad. They were not content to be merely spectators; they had to be at the heart of the action.

The truth of Jesus' words was plain to see for the early Church. He would 'build his church'. It all starts with 120 in the upper room. Peter then preaches the first sermon of the new Church and three thousand get added. Acts 2:47 says God added people daily (that's at least 365 a year!). In the end Luke gives up counting and says, 'thousands of Jews have believed'. Are you a season-ticket spectator in the stands or do you regularly make the team on the field? Maybe it's time for a change. Maybe it's time to nail your colours to the mast.

Continental

Did you know that there are more churches in the UK than all the supermarkets of the big chains put together? It's obvious that the Church is present in nearly every community. It's also obvious that just being there is not enough. It will take action on our part to see Jesus 'build his church' in our nation.

Coffee

Pop icon Boy George wrote of a recent trip to church that bored him silly: 'The Church badly needs a facelift because it's God's theatre on earth and he should be packing them in.' His conclusion is eye-opening, isn't it?

Orange Juice

If we claim to know him and don't obey him, we are lying and the truth isn't in our hearts.

(1 JOHN 2:4)

LIVING A LIE?

The Big Breakfast

I have often heard it said that young people today don't know how to worship. Rubbish! Just one look at the bedroom wall of most teenagers will show you how well they worship pop stars, fashion icons and sporting heroes alike. We all need heroes to follow and role models to emulate – it's how we were made.

When I was twelve, Johan Cruyff was captain of Holland in football's World Cup finals. His amazing footwork and goal-scoring talent made me want to be more like him. I rushed out and bought an orange football shirt, parted my hair to the left and copied his moves from the TV. I knew he was the greatest footballer in the world and I wanted to play like him.

You see, what I believed about Cruyff affected the way I behaved on the pitch. The same has to be true about God. What we really believe about God affects the way we live in the game of life. The calibre of our belief is measured by the quality of our behaviour. I don't want to live a lie. I want my everyday life to match up to my beliefs. I want to take God seriously and for others to see this lived out before them.

Continental

If you want to do a little self-test on your walk with God, first ask yourself if you behave in a way that shows your beliefs. Then ask someone else to see if your mouth matches your actions. This kind of pruning may be painful, but it's the only way to grow good fruit.

Coffee

Would you buy hair-restorer from a bald man? Of course not. His appearance undermines the product. Would your friends buy into Jesus? Only if your appearance matches up to your words. Take a look in the mirror today.

Orange Juice
He won't break off a bent reed or put out a dying flame.

(ISAIAH 42:3)

BREAKING POINT

The Big Breakfast
It doesn't take a prophet to tell you that life can so often be a bruising experience. Girls I have fallen head over heels in love with have unceremoniously dumped me. I have had friends murder my character with unwise words. I have wept till it hurts at the loss of loved ones, been unemployed, been kicked out of a church, failed all my exams and made the most stupid decisions possible.

Maybe you've had similar experiences. You once knew what it was to stand strong and tall, but now you are bent double and bruised by the pain of life. Maybe you still feel that way today. The memories of previous traumas, and the tumours that still eat away at your soul, cause you to hang your head and let your shoulders drop.

If you feel at breaking point, you can be sure that even when others fail you or your own stupid lifestyle choices let you down, Jesus won't break you. He will only build you up again. His voice will be one of concern and care, not condemnation. His love will not end in hurt but in healing.

Why run away from that kind of support? Why leave him out in the cold when he wants to welcome us back into the warm?

Continental
It seems to me that the older you get the easier it is to let the flame of faith smoulder away. Do you remember being proud of a faith that burnt bright? They called you a fanatic and you didn't care. What was it that caused the flame to become a flickering light? Take Paul's advice and begin again to 'fan into flame the gift that is within you'.

Coffee
Think about *The Message*'s new spin on this verse, which says of Jesus: 'He won't walk over anyone's feelings, he won't push you into a corner.'

Orange Juice

We gladly suffer, because we know that suffering helps us to endure. And endurance builds character which gives us a hope that will never disappoint us.

(ROMANS 5:3–4)

FAT SHEEP SURVIVE

The Big Breakfast

How daft can you get? Who ever heard of being glad about suffering? Where can you find the good in the bad? How can hard times be something to be thankful for?

I once stayed with a Lebanese family in Beirut. Before the civil war my host had worked in finance and had travelled regularly on business to the Scottish Highlands. I asked him how life in the city of Beirut differed from that in the Scottish hills. 'Easy,' he said. 'It's the sheep!' He explained that his overriding memory of the craggy Scottish hillsides was of how fat the sheep were compared to the skinny, lop-eared versions that populate the parched hills of his country. 'Put a sheep from Beirut on a mountainside near the lochs and it would be dead by the next morning,' he said. And he was right. The harsh Scottish winters had somehow toughened the sheep for survival.

We rejoice in life's storms because each one produces the perseverance to weather the next one as the very character of Jesus is pressed into us. Spending your days merely roaming the sun-drenched hillsides of life and choosing to escape the dark clouds will eventually lead to ruin at the first sight of a

Continental

Do you know how a precious and rare pearl is formed in an oyster? I am told that it's the constant grinding and irritation of tiny grains of sand that get inside its shell. Instead of rejecting it, the oyster encases it in layers of beauty to form a pearl. Will you let your life today grind you down or will you allow it to produce beauty in your character?

Coffee

C.S. Lewis once wrote, 'God whispers in our conscience, speaks in our silence and shouts in our sufferings. It is his megaphone to rouse a deaf world.'

Orange Juice

But when he was still a long way off, his father saw him and felt sorry for him. He ran to his son and hugged and kissed him.

(LUKE 15:20)

REMIND YOU OF ANYBODY?

The Big Breakfast

I was so sure that the flight I was on was going to be my last. It was with an airline I'd never heard of, on a plane that looked as if it had been made by a *Blue Peter* presenter. It was so old that I had to sit next to the rear gunner! I held my breath as the thing lumbered slowly down the runway and up into the Middle Eastern sky. I was travelling with an Arab Christian friend to Jordan, where he was to be reunited with the family he hadn't seen for a few weeks.

We eventually touched down – three times – and bundled hurriedly out of the plane, through baggage reclaim and towards the exit. My friend must have been excited about seeing his wife and two young boys again but he never showed it. 'I'll take the bags,' I offered, 'you run on ahead.'

He dropped his case and turned to me sternly. 'Arab fathers never run.' In that moment, the weight of what the prodigal son's father did came crashing into me. He broke with all tradition and did what no father with dignity would ever do; he ran and ran, working up a sweat in the sun. He dispensed with a formal handshake and threw his arms around his boy publicly. He even cut short the lad's well-prepared repentance speech with the order to prepare a banquet. Remind you of anybody?

Continental

When my eldest son was a baby, he once covered every available space on his face, hands and body with a rapidly melting chocolate ice cream. Then he began to choke. I didn't hesitate – I didn't stop to clean him up, I gave no thought to my own appearance, I just lifted him up, cleared the blockage and held him tight, with all his mess pressed against my clean white shirt. Remind you of anybody?

Coffee

'If you kept record of sins, no one could last long. But you forgive us' (Psalm 130:3). Reminds me of the Master. Worship him.

Orange Juice

Our LORD and Ruler, your name is wonderful everywhere on earth! … I often think of the heavens your hands have made … then I ask, 'Why do you care about us humans?'

(PSALM 8:1, 4)

WELLY WALKS

The Big Breakfast

I've had such fun today. I've learnt to recapture the wonder of life from my 18-month-old son Nathan. My wife is out of town visiting her family and so I've had our two boys all to myself. The sun was warm despite an early-morning downpour. We decided on a 'welly walk' around the grounds of Upton House, a stately home not far from where we live.

For Nathan it was a day of 'firsts', each new discovery accompanied with jubilant squeals of delight. First it was the feel of running his little hands over a damp, beautifully mown lawn. Then his brother presented him with a trapped butterfly that tickled his smiling face as it flew to freedom. Moment by moment his little eyes grew wider with a joy-overload as he splashed his wellies through the puddles, caught his reflection in the clear water of a pond and then tottered off down a stony path with his hands clasped behind his back like a patrolling headmaster.

He and his brother fell into a contented sleep on the way home, leaving me to ponder how I could recapture that childlike innocence. I felt as if I had lost the wonder of life. How much more dynamic would my worship be if I 'thought about the heavens God's hands have made' more often?

Continental

The next time I go to worship I may just pull on my wellies, squeal in wonder at those beautiful God moments and then splash about in the puddles of the Father's love that our church community demonstrates so well.

Coffee

Affirm with me: 'LORD God, you stretched out your mighty arm and made the sky and the earth. You can do anything' (Jeremiah 32:17).

Orange Juice

You are the one who put me together inside my mother's body ... Nothing about me is hidden from you! I was secretly woven together ... but with your own eyes you saw my body being formed. **(PSALM 139:13–16)**

THE MAKING OF A MAN

The Big Breakfast

When Debbie was pregnant with our first son, we went for our 12-week scan at the local hospital. The doctor in the long white coat spread unnecessary amounts of what looked like hair gel on Mum's tum and began the scan. He showed no emotion. The total opposite was true of the doting parents. You could have wedged a pair of coat hangers into our mouths as we watched the images flicker up on to the screen. I could see the head and the little heart beating, the tiny fingers and tiny toes. I felt a tear of joy and wonder trickle down my cheek as I gazed in amazement at this 12-week-old baby who was now fully formed and ready to grow.

'Everything is normal,' concluded the white coat.

'No it isn't,' I insisted. He shot me a stare. 'I have just peered into my wife's stomach and seen my 12-week-old child. That's not normal – it's utterly amazing!'

God didn't blink and you were made. He took time over you, 'putting you together inside your mother's body'. He took time out for some quality control and let 'his own eyes see your body being formed'. I even think he allowed a tear of joy to trickle down his holy cheek in amazement and wonder. Make you feel special?

Continental

Answer me this: there are six billion people alive on planet earth right now. How does God keep on managing to make every one so different? I mean, there can't be many more ways of arranging a nose, two eyes and a mouth. Yet he throws away the pattern every time and starts knitting again from scratch.

Coffee

'I praise you because of the wonderful way you created me. Everything you do is marvellous! Of this I have no doubt' (Psalm 139:14).

Orange Juice

Praise the God and Father of our Lord Jesus Christ for *the spiritual blessings* that Christ has brought us from heaven.

(EPHESIANS 1:3)

JOYS-R-US!

The Big Breakfast

One Saturday, a few Christmases ago, I trudged wearily through the winter snow to the megastore Toys-R-Us. I'd gone with a good friend, his seven-year-old son Jonathon and a huge crowd. Jonathon's dad said he could have anything he wanted from the store as long as it came to no more than the five pounds. The boy ran off like a hungry lion, devouring every sparkly new toy he could feast his eyes on. He soon came back and tried to bargain for a higher allowance, but to no avail. The imposed limit meant it took him hours to decide. Eventually he decided on a little £4.99 working model of C3PO from the *Star Wars* films, the closest thing to the £5 limit. Value for money!

The 'spiritual blessings' that Paul was describing are like our heavenly Father taking his kids to his megastore of good things, but unlike an earthly father he says, 'All this, every good thing you can see; it's all yours because of Jesus.' No limits here, no sale items or returns, just pure spiritual blessings from the heavenly realms.

Continental

Paul wrote of these spiritual blessings from a prison cell. I spent today in a prison with a prison officer from our church. There was no hope there, only chains of sadness. Yet even Paul's chains couldn't stop him getting excited about his blessings. Don't be a whinger today – change your perspective and watch your chains drop off!

Coffee

Stop right now, before the rest of this day unfolds, and thank God for his heavenly blessings. The list seems endless. Undeserved grace, eternal life, freedom from guilt, healing from pain, a new purpose to life, sweet sweet forgiveness ...

Orange Juice

Before the world was created, God had Christ choose us to live with him, and to be his holy, innocent and loving people. God was kind and decided that Christ would choose us to be God's own adopted children. *(EPHESIANS 1:4–5)*

FROM ORPHAN TO HEIR

The Big Breakfast

Here Paul captures the dynamite truth of the gospel that exploded into a Bethlehem cattle shed two thousand years ago. Let me quote these verses again from the Bloomin' Obvious Bible (Colour Pictures Edition):

Continental

My friends Chris and Ruby were childless for fifteen years. Just yesterday they flew back from Manila with their newly adopted daughter Michelle. You should have seen the unstoppable joy on their faces. Remember today your heavenly Father's joy the day he picked you up from a foreign land and brought you home.

You got picked before God ever flung up a star into the night sky or rolled out a mountain range. With no other motivation but sheer, gratuitous love he picked you out among many orphaned souls to eat at his table; not as a visitor or a temporary guest but as a son or a daughter. He did it because he wanted to and because adopting you meant that nothing else in the history of the universe he had created could ever give him so much pleasure. Not even England beating Germany on penalties.

He is really glad to have chosen you. Despite your tantrums and selfish choices, despite your blatant rebellion, he is still proud of you. He still thinks you were worth every drop of blood that spilt from the body of his only Son so that today you can call yourself his heir and adopted child.

Coffee

When God created Adam and Eve, his intention was to populate his planet with 'holy and innocent and loving people' (Ephesians 1:4). I still firmly believe that is his intention today. So as God's precious child, take a look at yourself again in the same way that he looks at you – holy and innocent.

Orange Juice

When you go without eating, don't try to look gloomy as those show-offs do … I can assure you that they already have their reward. Instead, comb your hair and wash your face. Then others won't know that you are going without eating. But your Father sees what is done in private, and he will reward you.

(MATTHEW 6:16–18)

HOLY ARROGANCE

The Big Breakfast

I know. You woke up this morning desperate for caffeine, opened this book for a word of encouragement, and what you got was 'go without eating'. What possible benefits can going without food really have?

Well, if it was a practice good enough for Jesus, it must therefore be worthy of some consideration. Matthew records: 'After Jesus had gone without eating for forty days and nights, he was very hungry.' Understatement of the decade or what? Most of us would struggle to let even a day go past without at least a bagel or a burger or a balti passing our lips.

I also believe that fasting is a kind of holy arrogance. It is saying to God that you are serious about an issue. So serious, in fact, that you're prepared to go without physical sustenance as you pray and that you won't accept no for an answer. What are you so desperate to catch God's attention with that you will add fasting to your petitioning? Whatever it is, the promise is clear. The Father will reward you as you fast and pray. Is it a day's meals you need to sacrifice, a week's TV or a month's shopping for the latest labels? You choose …

Continental

If fasting were an option for the Christian, Jesus would have said 'if you fast'. If fasting were a command, he would have said 'you *must* fast'. However, it was his assumption that real followers would fast, so he says 'when you fast'. Can he make the same assumption of you?

Coffee

The Methodist preacher William Bramhall said, 'The reason why Methodists in general do not live in this salvation is there is too much sleep, too much meat and drink, too little fasting and self-denial, too much preaching and hearing and too little self-examination and prayer.' Where will you stand?

Orange Juice

Happiness makes you smile; sorrow can crush you.

(PROVERBS 15:13)

SACRED LAUGHTER

The Big Breakfast

I drove home today from what proved to be a very difficult and intense meeting. My mind was racing with words both said and unsaid. I could almost feel my heart aching in my chest. My spirit had been dragged down, if not a little crushed. God knew that I needed to crack a smile on my face and get a clearer perspective. I am sure God invented laughter as one of life's little shock-absorbers. I switched on the radio. It was a satirical news show. I laughed like a hyena all the way to my front door.

I can see a whole bunch of humour in the Bible – not least Jesus telling the apocryphal tale of Mr and Mrs Raven building a barn (Matthew 6:26) or the almost Pythonesque picture of fat camels squeezing through the eye of a needle (Mark 10:25)! And how about the comic irony of Joseph teaching the creator of the world how to hold a hammer? The sad thing is, so many Christians have had their humour gland surgically removed by the Church. We really are boring people to hell. Don't run from the lighter moments of life. Embrace them tightly and discover a God of life and laughter right at their centre.

Continental

American pastor and author Charles Swindoll said of laughter, 'I think it is often just as sacred to laugh as it is to pray or preach or witness.' I agree with him. I mean, when cheese gets its picture taken, what does it say?

Coffee

Queen Victoria is famed for saying, 'We are not amused.' Is that true of you? Here's one that might check out how rusty your smile has become.

Q: How can you spot a Christian fish? A: It's got a car stuck to its backside!

Orange Juice
Be still and know that I am God.

(PSALM 46:10 NIV)

RELAX...

The Big Breakfast
I am a big fan of noise and frantic activity. I grew up in 'loud London', where I spent my days in the hustle and bustle of an inner-city school playground and my evenings either playing football, watching football or listening to music welded on 10. I love noise. Or should that read, 'I LOVE NOISE'?

If truth were told, the thought of 'being still' frightens me to death. Is this really the only way to know God?

The Hebrew word here (*raphah*) means 'relax'. Now that I can do. One commentator suggests it means to cease striving. So the way to know God is to relax, to cease striving, to slow down.

When did you last do that? When did you last drive under the speed limit, not rush your supper, switch off your mobile phone for a day or read a book in a piping hot bath? If we don't do these kinds of things we run the risk of falling deeper into the tyranny of the busy and continually struggling with stress.

Worse still, we run the risk of not knowing God. You have my permission to find a space to relax today. Then you will know that he really is your God.

Continental
I dug this out of an old book I was given. It's a few lines written by an old friar near the end of his life. 'If I had my life to live over again … I would relax, I would limber up, I would be sillier than I have been this trip … I would ride on more merry-go-rounds. I'd pick more daisies.'

Coffee
Join in Augustine's prayer of old: 'O Lord, you have made us for yourself, and our heart is restless until it finds rest in you.'

Orange Juice

When (the disciples) landed, they saw a fire of burning coals there with fish on it, and some bread ... Jesus said to them, 'Come and have breakfast.'

(JOHN 21:9–12 NIV)

BREAKFAST WITH GOD'S SON

The Big Breakfast

My favourite time of day to meet with people is over breakfast. I love the smell of fresh toast and coffee, mixed with warm conversation, while watching the sun crack open the sky on a brand new day. I have breakfasted with family, good friends, politicians, colleagues, reporters, actors, footballers, even a tramp on Marylebone Station in London. But can you imagine breakfasting with the world's creator? What would you say to him? What might he say to you? Who would pick up the tab?

The disciples were gripped with disappointment. Their Messiah had died and with him their hopes and their dreams. They had gone back to their old way of life – fishing. And on their first trip out they caught nothing. Then the stranger's advice from the lakeside hauls them a huge bounty. Suddenly they are full of beans and scrambling ashore to find a Saviour who is very much alive and cooking them fish butties for breakfast. His invitation to them still stands for us today and tomorrow and the days after that: 'Come and have breakfast with me.' Worth getting up for, eh?

Continental

Breakfast with God. Not just a clever book title but a definite daily reality. No matter that your life is frantic and full of failure or fear, he still wants to cook breakfast and lay a place for you at the table. Tell him what's on your mind and ask for his companionship today. Pass the butter please ...

Coffee

I find it quite ironic that this story tells of a carpenter shouting instructions from the shore to a bunch of fishermen. Listen for the advice from heaven today, but remember that it often comes from the most unlikely of sources.

Orange Juice

The LORD alone gives and takes. Praise the name of the Lord!

(JOB 1:21)

WHAT SPILLS OUT?

The Big Breakfast

Why was Job praising the name of the Lord? He was a very wealthy man who had lost his servants and his many cattle in a dramatic raid and firestorm. He had been blessed with ten kids, and they had all died in a freak tornado storm (Job 1:13–19). He had lost the lot, and gained some rather nasty boils into the bargain that even Clearasil couldn't shift (Job 2:7).

What was his reaction? Was it to join the ranks of the power-whingers? Did he sign up to the 'why me?' brigade? Not Job. He came to God empty-handed and vulnerable. Naked, in fact – totally dependent on him. Then he began to praise his name.

At first glance this paints a picture to me of Job as some kind of spiritual superman. I could never be like that. But Job was a man just like you and me – yet it was said of him that he was 'a truly good person, who respected God and refused to do evil' (Job 1:1). It proves to me that this kind of attitude of the soul can be attained. I can demonstrate my trust in God right at the heart of chaos and calamity.

What spills out of you when the pain of life really starts to bump in?

Continental

If whingeing was an Olympic sport, I am sure some of us would be gold medallists. Moaning for many has become a regular pastime. Whether it's our local politician or our local preacher, we spend more time whingeing about them rather than worshipping our God.

Coffee

Paul's advice to the church in Philippi was to 'do *everything* without grumbling or arguing' (Philippians 2:14). Get the drift? Everything. Yep, everything.

Orange Juice

The Lord explained: 'Jeremiah, I am the LORD God. I rule the world and I can do anything.'

(JEREMIAH 32:26–7)

MISSION POSSIBLE

The Big Breakfast

Put your finger in this page, close your eyes for a minute and think about the things that just seem impossible right now.

Now imagine you are about 14 years old. Your boyfriend Joe is due round any moment, and a heavenly presence fills your room. The angelic being has got an important message: 'God on high has decreed that he wants to borrow your womb for his son. When he is born, give him the name Jesus.' You are naturally a little shocked at the news. Especially since you have never, you know… So how can this be? Besides, what will your folks say? And Joe, he'll go nuts. You put this to the angel with a strong sense of urgency. Don't fret, comes the reply, 'nothing is impossible with God' (Luke 1:37).

So answer the question. Is anything too difficult for God? Absolutely not! If he can encase himself in a set of bones, travel through time and space and then spend nine months in the womb of a teenage virgin called Mary, he can make possible your impossible. I have no idea what that is for you right now, but I do know one thing: nothing, and absolutely nothing, is impossible for God.

Continental

My friend Jeff used to work with tough-nosed London street kids. He sometimes worried about the day ahead as he walked from his home to the youth centre next to the Courage brewery. One morning he noticed the neon brewery sign flickering. It read 'Take Courage', as he pondered a God who said that nothing was impossible for him.

Coffee

Jesus said, 'No chance at all, if you think you can pull it off by yourself. Every chance in the world if you trust God to do it' (Luke 18:27 *The Message*). Get yourself out of the driving seat and let him take the wheel today.

Orange Juice
What do you know about tomorrow? How can you be so sure about your life? It is nothing more than mist that appears for only a little while before it disappears.

(JAMES 4:15)

FRAGILE LIFE

The Big Breakfast
Life is more fragile than we think. I'm reminded of a tense train journey from Banbury to London Marylebone. On the previous day in Paddington, just a few miles from my destination, two commuter trains collided at high speed, killing over 30 people and creating one of Britain's worst rail disasters.

The businessman who sat opposite me was reading a newspaper. The headline was simple and filled the front page: 'Commuters die on their way to work'. Nobody who had boarded that train to London would have dreamt it to be their last journey. It made my journey particularly strained. I gazed around to see a train carriage full of people all reading the same newspaper headlines. It seemed that one of the drivers had jumped a red light, with horrific consequences. We all travelled in an eerie silence.

James catches the mood well when he describes you and me as 'mist that appears for only a little while'. Take time to pause and thank God for giving you this day. For many it will be their last; for many today was never afforded to them. But for you, God has given you another day to live. Life is precious. Learn not to waste a moment.

Continental
An old youth leader of mine tried to explain how our lives now compare with eternal life. He asked me to hold an end of cotton between my thumb and forefinger. He then unravelled the rest of the reel around the room. It took him an age. Compared with life beyond the grave, he said, our lives now are as short as the bit between my fingers.

Coffee
'Lord, I don't take this day for granted. I won't wish it to end until I've managed to thank you for it over and over again.' Pray that prayer again over lunch, over supper, and before your head hits the pillow tonight. Be thankful!

Orange Juice

People who are like these little children belong to the kingdom of God. I promise you that you cannot get into God's kingdom unless you accept it the way a child does.

(MARK 10:15)

JUMP FROM THE TOP STEP

The Big Breakfast

I think some nursery rhymes should be banned. Have you thought about the words to some of them? Remember this line from 'Goosey Goosey Gander'? 'And if you see an old man standing unawares, grab him by the left leg and pull him down the stairs.' And we wonder why we live in such a violent society today!

I am convinced that our faith needs to become less childish and more childlike. There is a distinct difference. We need that simple naive acceptance of God's love for us mixed with our total trust in him. My two-year-old will launch himself off the stairs into my arms, never thinking that I could possibly drop him. I am his father and, in his eyes, his daddy will always catch him without fail. Simple childlike faith.

If only I could recapture some of that same reckless abandonment to my heavenly Father. Why is it that I hold back so much and so often? I miss out on the adventure and thrill of diving into the arms of my creator and squealing with delight as he holds me close.

Continental

Remember the tale about the emperor who had no clothes? It took a little scruffy lad to be uninhibited enough to say what everyone was thinking. Can you start to dismantle some of that grown-up safety net that so often gets wrapped around your view of God and the Church? Because unless you do *you cannot get into God's kingdom.*

Coffee

The writer Randall Jarrell is quoted as saying, 'One of the most obvious facts about grown-ups, to a child, is that they have forgotten what it is like to be a child.' Lose the confusion and accept again today that your perfect Father in heaven loves you, his very special child. Dive once more into his open arms.

Orange Juice

Then the ones who pleased the Lord will ask, 'When did we give you something to eat or drink?' … The king will answer, 'Whenever you did it for any of my people … you did it for me.'

(MATTHEW 25:37–40)

THE NORMAL CHRISTIAN LIFE

The Big Breakfast

From reading this story that Jesus tells about separating the sheep and the goats, it's clear that we need to think carefully about the criteria for finding favour with the Almighty. The story tells of a time when Jesus will separate people 'as shepherds separate their sheep from their goats' (Matthew 25:32). The favourable ones are not necessarily the successful church leaders or clever Bible scholars. They are not the greatest preachers or most poetic songwriters. They are not even the people who feel it their 'Christian duty' to do a weekly soup run or organize a jumble sale for worthy causes.

The righteous people, the ones who miss out on eternal punishment and find eternal life (Matthew 25:46) are the ones who feed the hungry without thinking about it. They welcome strangers quite naturally. They see the poor and naked and don't think twice about buying them the best set of clothes available. They even willingly take time out to visit the drug-pusher, the prostitute or the thief, living behind bars.

When did your faith last get close enough to the poor to smell their need and hear the silent cry of their inner souls? You say you love them, but have they ever heard you say it? Have they ever seen it in action?

Continental

Authentic followers of Christ assume that cleaning up the vomit of the user, cradling the diseased and dying or sacrificing what they have for those who have little is a natural, expected part of their daily lives. They would live this way without even thinking about it. They don't need a preacher to motivate them to live this way. You would hear them say, 'Surely that's the way every Christian lives, isn't it?' Is it?

Coffee

We must grasp this. Feeding hungry faces is as much worship as singing praise songs, if not more. Why? Because in both you will see the face of Jesus gazing back at you.

Orange Juice
As a deer gets thirsty for streams of water, I truly am thirsty for you, my God.

(PSALM 42:1)

CHECK YOUR PANTS

The Big Breakfast
A few years back, I preached in an old Pentecostal church. Just before I spoke, the worship band led people in a series of worship songs, the final one being the old classic, 'As the deer *pants* for water so my soul longs after you'. The worship leader paused midway through this song to encourage us all to speak out our prayers. One elderly lady's prayer left me doubled over with pain as I attempted to hold the tears of laughter back. 'O Lord,' she said, 'some of us only have short *pants* tonight, others I know have only long *pants* … yet for me, Lord, I honestly don't have any *pants* at all.' I just managed to pull myself together in time.

The Psalmist's words from centuries past ring loud today with this question. How thirsty are you to know God today? How parched is your palate and how chapped are your lips? Was opening the pages of this book a real chore today or are you serious about taking in another long, cool, thirst-quenching drink from his Spirit? If you look into your soul this morning, what is it you really thirst after?

Continental
Where do you go to drink from God? Whether it is alone with this book or in a small group of like-minded believers, or even church on a Sunday, make sure you drink often — certainly more than once a week. If you are thirsty, you stop to drink at least once a day. If you don't, you just dry up.

Coffee
You can hear the desperate heart cry of the writer in the verse that follows. 'In my heart, I am thirsty for you, the living God. When will I see your face?' Have that same passion to find God today and every day.

Orange Juice
One night ... the LORD God appeared to him in a dream and said, 'Solomon, ask for anything you want and I will give it to you.'

(1 KINGS 3:5)

HOMER SIMPSON AND THE ALMIGHTY

The Big Breakfast
One of my favourite theologians is Homer Simpson. In one *Simpsons* episode he decides to give up on church, and that night the Almighty himself comes to visit in a dream. I wonder if sometimes we underestimate the power of God speaking to us in dreams. It is a very biblical occurrence. Imagine you, like Solomon, had a heavenly dream where God, sounding a bit like the legendary genie of the lamp, offers you a chance to ask him for anything you wish. What would your answer be?

Solomon's answer is incredible. He asks God: 'Please make me wise and teach me the difference between right and wrong' (1 Kings 3:9). God's response is equally spectacular: 'You could have asked to live a long time or to be rich. Or you could have asked for your enemies to be destroyed. Instead, you asked for wisdom to make right decisions. So I'll make you wiser than anyone who has ever lived or ever will live' (1 Kings 3:12).

As God is always reckless in his affection for his children, he goes on to promise Solomon, 'You'll be rich and respected' (1 Kings 3:13).

Continental
So how do we get wisdom? Is it reserved for the spiritual elite or can we all share in its benefit? The book of James tells us that the start of the process is simple. 'If any of you need wisdom, you should *ask* God, and it will be given to you. God is generous and won't correct you for asking.'

Coffee
Feel the urgency of this proverb, and let it stir your soul into action: 'The best thing about Wisdom is Wisdom herself; good sense is more important than anything else' (Proverbs 4:7).

Orange Juice

They gave as much as they could afford and even more, simply because they wanted to.

(2 CORINTHIANS 8:3)

STOP PRAYING

The Big Breakfast

We forgot the collection baskets in church last Sunday so we had to use a pot from the kitchen. The collection was a noisy affair!

I used to preach quite regularly in a Pentecostal church. The first time I witnessed their style of collection, it amazed me. The entire congregation lined up in front of the pastor with their offerings and they were quite at liberty to put notes in and take change out. Sometimes the pastor would call for people to line up again if he felt the bag was too empty.

It doesn't matter how you give to God as long as you give as much as you are able, and beyond. Be honest with yourself. Do you give regularly? If the answer is no, then start. It's a biblical command and not an option for the authentic follower of Christ. Now take some time to figure out how much you are able to give. Finally, don't give the figure you have just written down or thought of – give more. Don't fool yourself about needing to pray about it first. The best way to start is by being generous in the giving of your time, possessions and finances. Then and only then will your spirit become generous. It seems to me that when we give *even more* the adventure really begins.

Continental

Archbishop Temple once said, 'The last place that gets converted on a man is his pocket.' How easy it is to talk a good game when it comes to our commitment to God. How much harder it is to demonstrate it with our actions.

Coffee

'The group of followers all felt the same way about everything. None of them claimed that their possessions were their own, and they shared everything they had… no one went in need of anything' (Acts 4:32–4). Is this true of your church?

Orange Juice

He came into his own world, but his own nation did not welcome him.

(JOHN 1:11)

SPEECHLESS

The Big Breakfast

I can recall three moments in life that really left me speechless. The first was when I was only eight years old and my dad took me to my first professional soccer match. I can't remember too much about the game, only the feeling of being speechless as I walked through the turnstile and up into the electric atmosphere of a roaring crowd waiting for the game to begin.

The second event that left me in that same speechless state came a few summers back. A good friend bought me a ticket to see the British Formula 1 Grand Prix at Silverstone. It was the roar of the engines this time that took my breath away and gave me a memory to treasure for ever.

The third was when I read this verse for the first time and realized the magnitude of what God did to rescue me. The thought of God coming to his own creation, the people he made, his sons and daughters, with the answer to this life and hope for the next – and we chose not to receive him, but to string him up.

It steals your breath to think of a God who picked up his kids in his arms, went to kiss them with his love, and all they did was to wriggle free and run off.

Continental

It would break my heart to have my two boys turn their backs on me. It would crush me beyond hope to have them slam the door on my affection and leave me out in the cold. It literally broke the Father's heart when we murdered his Son.

Coffee

What of us who have received him? 'Yet some people accepted him and put their faith in him, so he gave them the right to be the children of God. They were not God's children by nature or because of any human desires. God himself was the one who made them his children' (John 1:12–13).

Orange Juice
You have been teaching all over Jerusalem.

(ACTS 5:28)

WHAT'S YOUR BHAG?

The Big Breakfast
I love reading business and leadership books. My favourite book of the moment is *Built To Last* by James Collins and Jerry Porras. A good friend gave it to me, and I simply couldn't put it down. One chapter is entitled 'BHAGs – Big Hairy Audacious Goals'. It suggests that people who make their lives count always have goals that are *big, hairy and audacious*.

It made me question what my goals were for the task God has given me. Were they big enough? It came to me like a bolt out of the blue when I read what the high priest said to the early church leaders in Jerusalem. He commanded them to stop preaching about Jesus because they had filled Jerusalem with their teaching. A quarter of a million people lived in the city, and everyone knew what the Church stood for – parents, newspaper editors, business gurus, prostitutes, drug addicts, alcoholics, homosexuals, schoolchildren, nurses, shopkeepers. Even those from other faiths knew. I realized that hardly anyone in my town knows why we exist as a community of believers. My BHAG is to change that in the next five years. What's the passion that drives you?

Continental
My goal is that all the 16,000 homes in my town and its 40,000 inhabitants will know about the kingdom of God because of what our church teaches. Sure it's big, if not a touch audacious. You could even class it hairy! But it's a dream that creates a passion in me that often keeps me awake at night.

Coffee
In 1960 American President John F. Kennedy presented his BHAG: 'within the next decade to place a man on the moon and bring him back again'. He died in 1963, but his dream came true in 1969. Big dreams don't depend on those who dreamt them in the first place. Tell someone your dreams today, before they fade away.

Orange Juice

How great is the love the Father has *lavished* on us, that we should be called children of God. And that is what we are!

(1 JOHN 3:1 NIV)

IT'S SPREAD THICKLY

The Big Breakfast

'Lavished'. What a great word – so opulent that it should stand alone.

How great is the love the Father has
LAVISHED
upon us.

It's such a big word. It's the kind of word that should be taken for lunch to the Ritz Hotel, dressed in an Italian suit and entertained at the opera in Vienna. You can't even say the word without raising the tone of your voice along with accompanying hand gestures. God is no cheap lover. He has lavished his love and affection on you.

Let me explain it another way. My mum and dad are very different, especially when it comes to breakfast-table habits. My dad spreads the butter carefully across the surface of the toast, ensuring every corner is covered. He then measures the jam out precisely before spreading it evenly on top of the butter. My mum is different – the creative type. She dollops on the butter, pushes it around the toast a little, then spoons out a lavish portion of jam. Yum! I always preferred it when my mum lavished breakfast on me as a kid.

Continental

How much do you think God loves you today? This verse says that his love doesn't dribble out like a leaky tap. It pours out from heaven like the water cascading over Niagara Falls. His love for you is 'spread thickly'. Make sure you take a bite at the start of the day today.

Coffee

'We are never left short-changed. We can't round up enough containers to hold everything God generously pours into our lives through the Holy Spirit' (Romans 5:5 *The Message*). Let your heart worship this outrageously generous Saviour.

Orange Juice

When he saw the crowds he felt sorry for them. They were confused and helpless, like sheep without a shepherd.

(MATTHEW 9:36)

RELENTLESS PURSUIT OF THE LOST

The Big Breakfast

We need to recapture a sense of how God feels about 'the lost'. One of the most eventful routines in our family life is the weekly trip to the supermarket. It takes all our efforts to fill the trolley with goods while hanging on to two kids. One day we lost our four-year-old son, Matthew. A chocolate bar in the shape of a light sabre had caught his eye and we got a couple of aisles ahead of him. When we noticed we were an offspring short, what do you think we did?

You couldn't imagine us saying to the manager, 'We come in most Mondays, so if you find him we'll pick him up then.' No. Debbie bellowed his name while I ran up and down the aisles, shoving people out of the way. Eventually we found him, embraced him fondly, then berated him!

If a shepherd lost one of his sheep, he would engage in that same passionate pursuit. That is what God thinks about those who don't know him. So why is it that the Church lets 'the lost' slip so easily by, without even a simple word of hope?

Continental

In Britain, 1,500 people join the Church every week, but the bad news is that 1,600 die each week. The even more depressing news is that around 80,000 people leave the Church each year. Whatever country we live in, lost people matter to God, so they must start to matter to us.

Coffee

'Show your power, O Lord'. There are two lines from this song that always stir my heart: 'We ask not for riches but look to the cross./And for our inheritance give us the lost.' Maybe it's time to stop asking God for *riches* and to start asking for *the lost* people in your world to become your inheritance.

Orange Juice

My soul finds rest in (waits in silence for) God alone.

(PSALM 62:1 NIV)

WAITING ROOM?

The Big Breakfast

Being an activist, my frequent prayer is the well-loved plea, 'Lord give me patience, but could you hurry up about it, please.'

Do you ever ponder the really big questions in life? I still can't find an answer to what you have to plant to grow seedless grapes. But I do know this: we have developed the seedless variety because we have lost the ancient art of patience. Life is too frantic to pick out the pips, even though the ones with seeds are so much juicier!

For me, I would much rather do anything than wait, even if it's the wrong thing. Breakfasting with God can't be hurried. A bowl of muesli with the Messiah must never be rushed. How could we begin to think that a quick 'Morning, Lord' as we stuff a piece of toast in our mouths and rush headlong into the day could ever become the staple diet of the authentic follower of Christ?

Where does your soul find the rest it craves? Maybe it's in music, maybe it's in sport, or maybe it's in a summer's walk in the woods with friends. Wherever it may be, spend it with God, not running on ahead but waiting with him. You can't run and wait both at the same time.

Continental

My theological anorak buddies tell me that the word 'silence' here is best translated 'a quiet whisper'. What a great picture. We whisper our affection to God in a crowded world so that only he can hear, just as lovers whisper to each other in a restaurant. What will you whisper to him today?

Coffee

In verse 5 of the Psalm, David turns his declaration into a command to himself. Check out the punctuation: 'Find rest, O my soul, in (wait in silence for) God alone.' Get tough with your own inner life. Pursue patience.

Orange Juice

When you are angry, do not sin, and be sure to stop being angry before the end of the day. Don't give the Devil a chance to defeat you.

(EPHESIANS 4:26–7 NEW CENTURY VERSION)

GO ON ... GET MAD!

The Big Breakfast

You have my full permission to blow your stack once in a while – at the right time and for the right reasons, of course. Paul clearly says, 'when you are angry do not sin', so don't let anyone ever tell you that anger is wrong. It's a God-given emotion. Even Jesus got angry, especially with religious nutters (Matthew 23). The key is that in our anger we must not sin and we must resolve it 'before the end of the day'.

I've been trying to think about the times recently when I got justifiably angry and when anger got the better of me. I remembered a struggling gay friend who got thrown out of his church and felt kicked in the teeth by God. That got me angry. I also recalled a heated dispute in a crowded car park because somebody 'stole my place'. That time anger got me.

Think back over your journey this past week. When did you let anger get you? Maybe even now it's still eating away at you inside. Do you need to make a phone call to resolve it? Do it before the day is out, and you will stamp on the devil's foot that's been wedged in the door of your soul.

Continental

Sure, Jesus yelled at a few priests. He even lost his rag in the temple courts one day, but it was also recorded that 'All spoke well of him and were amazed at the gracious words that came from his lips' (Luke 4:22 NIV). Get the balance?

Coffee

The seventeenth-century clergyman Thomas Fuller once wrote, 'Anger is one of the sinews of the soul.' If we learn to harness its power from within, it is less likely to do damage from without.

Orange Juice

A lot of Samaritans in that town put their faith in Jesus because (of what) the woman had said.

(JOHN 4:39)

WHO WOULD YOU CHOOSE?

The Big Breakfast

OK. You've got the job. God asks you to find a top evangelist to tell the message of his love to your entire town, so you start by short-listing some potential candidates:

Your minister – too busy with the flower rota
Billy Graham – far too famous
Your old religion teacher – too busy sewing patches on his elbows
Martin Smith – too busy mumbling into a microphone
George Carey – too busy ironing his archbishop's outfit

At that moment, a woman from the local council estate wanders in, carrying some heavy shopping and an equally burdensome reputation for men she isn't married to.

'She's the one I want.'

'Sorry, Lord?' you cry.

'Melanie. She's the one I want. The one I really, really want.'

'But, Lord, she's not one of us. Do you know how many men she's been with? She's not even a Christian.'

Jesus chose such an evangelist. Don't ever think God can't use the unusable to bring entire towns face to face with himself.

Continental

When I first read this story of Jesus and the Samaritan woman it taught me a lot about how to share my faith (John 4). Tired and thirsty, Jesus met her in the midday sunshine at the local drinking well and asked her to help him get a drink. Maybe 'Can you help me?' really is better than 'Can I preach to you?'

Coffee

Sometimes our fear stops us speaking about God. 'What if I say the wrong thing?' Take heart. This woman's first words to the town were: 'Come and see a man who …' You can hear the response, 'Oh boy … not another one!'

Orange Juice

Nothing is as wonderful as knowing Christ Jesus my Lord. I have given up everything else and count it all as *rubbish*. All I want is Christ and to know that I belong to him.

(PHILIPPIANS 3:8—9)

TOILET TALK

The Big Breakfast

It seems to me that the Bible translators must have been suit-wearing, middle-class academics who never really came to grips with the language of the market-place. The Brethren gland within me understands their caution in using the word 'rubbish', but if you read this verse in the Authorised Version, it comes nearer the mark: 'I count it all dung.'

Now we're getting to the bottom of what Paul is trying to say. Now we see the priorities in his life. Let's revisit this verse again in the Bloomin' Obvious Bible (Colour Pictures Edition):

There ain't no competition here. What's the point in trying to keep up with the Joneses when the warehouse of heaven's best is bulging at the seams for me? Walking in step with the Master has meant ditching all the shiny stuff that slows me down. I reckon all those glittery bits are a pile of poo compared to a fresh delivery of Jesus to my soul and to my feet.

Excuse me, but when you see all that stuff for the crap it really is (not my words but the apostle Paul's), your Christ quota will go through the roof and following him becomes less duty and more joy.

Continental

Do you consider your career a loss compared to the greatness of knowing Christ? Do you consider your home, your bank balance, your wardrobe, your car or your new DVD player in the same way? Tell me how exotic holidays can ever match up to basking in the brilliance of God's undeserved grace for you.

Coffee

This verse … a little bit strong? Feel offended? I think Paul's audience would have felt the same. I also think that they would have got the point. Have you?

Orange Juice

Mary ... who sat down in front of the Lord and was listening to what he said. Martha was worried about all that had to be done.

(LUKE 10:38—9)

IGNORE THE RODENT

The Big Breakfast

Pussycat, Pussycat, where have you been?
I've been up to London to look at the Queen!
Pussycat, Pussycat, what did you there?
I frightened a little mouse under her chair!

How often are God's subjects guilty of holding an audience with the King and getting distracted by something under his throne? Sure, they are often legitimate distractions. When will God answer my prayers about a partner? How can I invite the entire office to the Alpha course? Is that a new wig on my minister or is he just combing his hair forward?

Jesus and the crew drop in for tea and someone's got to cut the crusts off the cucumber sarnies. Mary waits and Martha works. She gets all steamed up about it. It's not that Martha was wrong to get busy, it was her attitude that let her down. 'Tell Mary to help me!' was her demand to Jesus.

I love the warmth and graciousness of Jesus' response. 'Martha, Martha, you are worried and upset about so many things, but only one thing is necessary. Mary has chosen what is best.' Don't miss out on what is best.

Continental

What are you worried about today? What's making you upset? I am sure they're all good, legitimate things. But don't let them distract you. Trade them in for a few minutes at the feet of Jesus. Rest your arms on his knees, gaze up into his eyes and listen to his conversation. Feeling better?

Coffee

Disciple, Disciple, where've ya bin?
I've been to Church to see the King!
Disciple, Disciple, what did you there?
I turned up late and mumbled a prayer!

Orange Juice

And God raised us up with Christ and seated us with him in the heavenly realms … in order that … he might show *the incomparable riches of his grace*, expressed in his kindness to us in Christ Jesus. *(EPHESIANS 2:6—8 NIV)*

AMAZING GRACE

The Big Breakfast

This 'grace' word is often used in church, in the Bible and in Graham Kendrick choruses. So it must be either an easy word to rhyme or a very important word. But what does it mean? And what are 'the incomparable riches of his grace'?

Philip Yancey recorded a true story that appeared in a Boston newspaper some years ago. A young woman had grown up poor and homeless but later found a good job and became engaged to a high-flying businessman. The couple confirmed the Hyatt Hotel for their reception. However, the man soon got cold feet and walked out on her. She had to cancel the hotel booking but stood to lose a great deal of money if she did. A thought came to her: 'Why don't I have this party anyway?' She set about inviting all the homeless she once knew to join her. So on that night, at a five-star hotel in Boston, those who normally scavenged cold pizza from rubbish skips ate the finest foods from hand-painted plates.

This is outrageous grace at its sweetest. It means us not getting what we deserve. In fact, it means us getting what we definitely don't deserve.

Continental

How do we get saved, then? By sitting in the front pew for 30 years? By regularly supporting 'whatsaname' on the mission field? By reading more books, listening to more sermons, or attending more prayer meetings? Or is it simply by the incomparable riches of his grace expressed in his kindness to us in Christ? Ask the thief on the cross!

Coffee

Allow the realization of this undeserved grace to crash into your soul more often, and you will walk more humbly, speak more gently and judge less harshly.

Orange Juice

The LORD God took a handful of soil and made a man. God breathed life into the man, and the man started breathing.

(GENESIS 2:7)

A WALKING MIRACLE

The Big Breakfast

A grand piano has 240 strings by which the world's finest concert pianist can produce a soul-churning melody. But the human ear that enables an audience to hear these sounds consists of 240,000 strings.

A TV camera has 60,000 photoelectric elements, which can capture any image. But the human eye, which functions unceasingly in any weather for around 70 years and has automatic focus, contains more than 137,000,000 elements.

A top-of-the-range, industrial IBM computer can handle the equivalent of one neurone of information at a time. But your brain has as many as 200 communicating pathways meeting in a single nerve cell or neurone. This means that in your brain there are 10,000 million neurones, each one serving as a mini microcomputer.

The Psalmist grasped something of this when he wrote of how fearfully and wonderfully made he was (Psalm 139:14). Take time to reflect, to stop and think. You are a walking miracle, a full-page colour advert to your Master's creativity and power. You may not feel like it today, but you are the pinnacle of his creation and he is proud of you.

Continental

I would go as far as to say that it is heresy for so many of our churches to be the dullest places on planet earth. What has happened to our creativity? You were made in the image of a creative God, the architect, designer and builder of this astonishing human frame of yours.

Coffee

'My Father, breathe again your life and your creativity into my soul and let me live once more. Let me dance as once I did, let me work, let me sing, let me play and let me pause again to praise your most holy of names. Amen.'

Orange Juice

If one of my followers sins against you, go and point out what was wrong. But do it in private, just between the two of you … But if that one refuses to listen, take along one or two others. *(MATTHEW 18:15-16)*

THE THREE-POINT PLAN

The Big Breakfast

I've done it. I've discovered the way to stop nations fighting, political parties accusing each other of scandal, close friends falling out with each other and churches splitting. We simply do what Jesus told his disciples to do in these verses. I've lived through the untruths that have caused a church to split and believers to ignore each other in the street. I've suffered at the hands of gossips. I'm sure you have, too.

So here is his three-point plan. First, *go* … It is your responsibility to make the first move and not to let it fester away, even if you don't think it's your fault! Second, *go and point out* to that person. Not to anyone else, but to that person. Don't tell anyone else before you tell them. In theory they are doing the same thing and you will meet in the middle to work it out *just between the two of you*. So you must keep it private. Third, if it is a real tough one to resolve, *take along one or two others*. Your aim must be to find a resolution, not to pick a fight. When Tony Blair became Prime Minister of Britain, he said, 'Enough of talking – it is time now to act.' When will you act on this principle?

Continental

Jesus goes on to say that 'if that person listens you have won back a follower'. Some of my deepest friendships are with people I have had to confront or people who have had to do the same with me. Some of my saddest memories are of people who chose to work up their anger rather than work out their differences.

Coffee

You may have seen the Second World War security poster that read 'Careless talk costs lives'. Maybe our churches would be safer places to be if that hung on our walls rather than next week's coffee rota. Watch your talk carefully today.

Orange Juice
Jesus replied, 'Come and see.' ... they went with him and saw where he lived. So *they stayed on for the rest of the day.*

(JOHN 1:39)

HANG OUT WITH JESUS

The Big Breakfast
Let your mind run riot with this one. The yet-to-be-appointed disciples get an invitation to spend the day with the Messiah. How would you keep a lid on that kind of excitement?

I was at a conference a few summers back when I met a former American Football player from Chicago called Jerry Root. Our short meeting made a deep and lasting impression on me. I wanted to be more like this man.

The following summer I was in Chicago. I plucked up courage and picked up the phone to Jerry (not expecting that he would even remember me). I was not prepared for his response. 'Duncan! I can't believe you're in town. Give me a few minutes to change my schedule and we can spend the day together.'

We spent the day on the campus of the theological college where he lectured, meeting the most interesting people. That night we sat around his kitchen table drinking wine and eating pizza with his family.

I'll never ever forget that day, just as the disciples of old would never have forgotten that day they spent with Jesus. Today is your opportunity.

Continental
Believe it or not, you are invited to spend this day with the Master. Oh yes, and the next day ... in fact, the whole week ... no, the whole month ... year ... decade. That was it ... FOR EVER.

Coffee
The promise of God is never to leave you or forsake you. Get it? He will *never, never, never, never, never, never, never,* forsake you. It's his promise to you. Get it now?

Orange Juice

The sheep know their shepherd's voice. He calls each of them by name and leads them out. When he has led out all his sheep, he walks in front of them, and they all follow, *because they know his voice.*   *(JOHN 10:3—4)*

VOICE MAIL

Continental

Fascinating Sheep Fact No. 223: When a sheep rolls over on to its back it can't get itself upright again. Many die like this, easy picking for a hungry fox. The only way it can get back on its feet is for someone to grab its coat and turn it over.

The Big Breakfast

My father-in-law Ken realized one of his life's ambitions when he left a jet-setting business in London and moved to the country. It was here that he and his wife began looking after sheep. I loved those crisp Christmas holiday mornings when we would wrap up warm and head off down the lane to count the sheep. Me in my scarf and bobble-hat and Ken looking the part in his Barbour jacket, flat cap and green farmers' wellies. When he yelled 'Sheep!' the flock would come running, and he would feed them sheep nuts, count them and pull any missing ones out of the hedgerows.

I looked after those sheep one summer, and even though I wore Ken's coat and hat, called them by the same name and offered them the same sheep nuts, they would always run away! Sometimes we wonder what God thinks about our life choices. Why does he seem to keep so quiet? Is that really his voice guiding me? Confusion rapidly sets in. Sheep know the shepherd's voice. No matter how it is dressed up, they always recognize the genuine article. Are you walking close enough to the Master today so that you can clearly distinguish his voice from a stranger's? His tone is filled with encouragement, discipline, grace and hope.

Coffee

Who do you know today who may have taken a tumble and could do with a call to put them back on their feet? Take some time to make that call.

Orange Juice

There is more happiness in heaven because of one sinner who turns to God than over ninety-nine good people who don't need to.

(LUKE 15:7)

PARTY TIME

The Big Breakfast

This is the first book I have ever written and is therefore very precious to me. I have written it all on my laptop computer. I have sweated over the words and themes while on long car, plane and train journeys. Sometimes it has flowed as I have sat around Steve's dining-room table while he is at work. Sometimes I have struggled with fresh insights as I have pulled over to the side of the road to jot down another possible idea on a scrap of paper that I always manage to lose anyway! But this is my baby. So you can imagine my bowel-shaking panic when my computer crashed last week and the man in the shop told me I had lost everything.

But can you imagine my heart-shattering joy when, a day later, the shop called me back to say they had managed to save a few things from my desktop, one of which was the *Breakfast with God* manuscript?

We are God's *magnum opus*, his inspired creation and his precious baby. No wonder there is one humdinger of a party in heaven when that which was lost gets found – or, as *The Message* puts it, when one sinner's life gets rescued.

Continental

Mary had been coming to our church for a few months before she got saved. I told her about the party in heaven that would go on late into the night because a precious daughter who was lost had been found. Mary turned up at my house the following night with a bottle of champagne. She wanted to carry on the party here on earth! And why not?

Coffee

Sometimes it is only when we recall how lost we once were that we can begin to appreciate the greatness of a God who relentlessly pursued us until we were found again. Say thank you to the Shepherd who went out on a limb to rescue you.

Orange Juice

Jesus asked the boy's father, 'How long has he been like this?'

(MARK 9:21)

HOW LONG HAS IT BEEN?

The Big Breakfast

Come on, be honest. Even if it's been a while since you've been honest with God or anyone else, be honest with yourself today. How long have you been like this? How long has the pain of that past experience been eating away at your soul? How long has that secret sin been haunting your every thought? So, how long — days, weeks, months, years? Surely it can't go on any longer? Surely something must happen soon to break the cycle? Surely now could be that time, couldn't it? The boy's father thought nothing could be done for the son he loved. The devil and his evil spirits had tormented this lad from birth. Even Jesus' disciples couldn't shift the problem.

But this man got honest. He got the problem out in the open and asked Jesus for help: 'Please have pity and help us if you can' (v. 22). Now is the time to get your trauma out in the open. Keeping it to yourself will be your ultimate downfall. And as you cry out for help today, heaven will cry out its promise to you. 'Anything is possible for someone who has faith' (v. 23). Remember this: mustard seed or mountain, it doesn't matter how big your faith is, it's where you place it that counts in the end.

Continental

I hate cutting the lawn. I try every trick in the book to get out of it. 'It's too wet. It's too dry. It's too short. It's too green. I'm too tired. I'm too busy.' Yet I have grown to realize that the longer I leave it the more difficult it is to deal with. How long have you been running?

Coffee

When will we learn the importance of keeping short accounts with God? When will we learn that being vulnerable and honest about our fears and failures will not harm us but save us? Commit your soul to setting the record straight. Now.

Orange Juice

Don't be like the people of this world, but let God change the way you think. Then you will know how to do everything that is good and pleasing to him.

(ROMANS 12:2)

SWIM AGAINST THE TIDE

The Big Breakfast

I grew up in London. When I was a kid, I would go Christmas shopping with Bernie, my 'best bud' from school. We would start at Piccadilly and work our way up to Marble Arch. Nothing too adventurous in that, I hear you say. But we would always go against the flow of people. It seemed to be an unwritten shopper's rule that you had to 'go with the flow'. Our little adventure was to swim against the tide and suffer the tutting of weary bargain-hunters and the incessant battering of over-filled shopping bags in the process. We would always win eventually and would reward ourselves with a McDonald's shake at Piccadilly Circus.

Following Christ in the third millennium demands that we must run counter to our culture. It means not letting this world squeeze us into its mould. Where have you found yourself being tempted to conform recently?

The adventure of our faith is to make a break from the norm and stop following the crowd. We must learn to ignore some of our culture's 'unwritten rules' and stick to the Master's plan. The result? I promise you this: the reward at the end is even sweeter than any strawberry shake!

Continental

I always thought that God's will for my life would be as boring as singing in the church choir. This verse reminds me that God actually wants to bring out the best in me. His will for my life is good, not bad; it's pleasing, not dull; it's perfect, and I could never improve on it.

Coffee

The Message brings this verse bang up to date: 'Don't become so well adjusted to your culture that you fit into it without even thinking. Instead, fix your eyes on God and you'll be changed from the inside out.'

Orange Juice

Listen! I'm standing and knocking at your door. If you hear my voice and open the door, I will come in and we will eat together.

(REVELATION 3:20)

FOOD, GLORIOUS FOOD!

The Big Breakfast

The same verse again – Bloomin' Obvious Version (Colour Pictures Edition):

Thump-Thump! – Are you deaf? It's me! I've been ringing the bell all day. Ding-Dong! – Look, I know you are in. My voice has gone all Tom Jones from bawling your name through the letterbox. Thump-Thump! – … If you can hear me, open up. I'm not going to rub it in – in fact, the reason I came round was to rub it all out! Let's pull up a chair and have a chat over an aubergine and lentil bake.

It's what Jesus never said that I find so fascinating about this famous verse from the last book of the Bible. He never said, 'Open your life to me and we'll hold a worship service where we will sing a few songs with a key change part way through that will make you spontaneously raise your hands.' He simply said, 'Open up, and we can eat a meal together,' which is exactly what friends do best. We must recapture this socially based approach to community life. I reckon that we need to build churches that sing together a little bit less and eat together a whole lot more. Less *Songs of Praise* and more *Ready, Steady, Cook*. Less 'washing in the river' and more 'washing up the dirties'.

Continental

Will a time ever come when the chairman of the catering committee will supersede the awesome status of church worship leader? Will we ever have full-time cooks as well as full-time pastors? Will we buy more cookery books than Christian music records?

Coffee

John Wimber said: 'People come to church for many reasons but stay for just one, and that's friendship.' Who do you need to invite round for supper this week?

Orange Juice

Other Levites – who were all skilled musicians – were in charge of carrying supplies and supervising the workers.

(2 CHRONICLES 34:12-13)

IF MUSIC BE THE FOOD OF LOVE ...

The Big Breakfast

As King Josiah began employing brickies to build the temple of the Lord, he made sure they were also skilled musicians. So why was that such an important qualification for this kind of job?

It's amazing what power music has and how it shapes today's culture. As I was flicking through a teenage magazine recently, an article on the power of music caught my eye. In a reader survey, it found that the place where young people turn first when life gets tough is not to their peers, parents or teachers but to their CD collection. I guess it was the same for all previous generations of young people.

So who is discipling this generation of music lovers? Where do teenagers get their values? The big hit of last summer repeated the chorus 'I wanna have sex on the beach', closely followed by 'Boom! Boom! Boom! Let me take you to my room.' They get their moral coding from the likes of Robbie Williams or George Michael or Madonna, to name but a few.

If music is such a powerful influence, then the Church needs many more skilled musos to write the new anthems of a generation increasingly hungry for lyrics filled with hope and tunes filled with passion.

Continental

As Chandler said to Phoebe in a recent episode of *Friends*, 'Gloria Estefan was right – eventually the rhythm is going to get you!' It's because God designed you that way. Don't resist it; rejoice in it.

Coffee

If you are one of this rare breed of quality writers and singers then don't give up the dream. If, like me, you are consigned to singing in the bath, then pray for the favour of God to be on them.

Orange Juice

I know everything that you have done, and you are not cold or hot. I wish you were either one or the other. But since you are lukewarm and neither hot nor cold, I will spit you out of my mouth. *(REVELATION 3:15-16)*

YOU MAKE
ME SICK

The Big Breakfast

'Knowing them inside and out, God looked at the church in Laodicea and said, "I am sick to death with you – you make me want to puke!"' (Bloomin' Obvious Version – Colour Pictures Edition).

I remember my parents, teachers and some football coaches saying something similar to me at various times when I was a kid. It wasn't that they didn't want the best for me. It wasn't even that my parents had stopped loving me. It was pure exasperation. Passion you can channel. Rebellion you can sort. Lukewarmness is a cancer that still has no cure.

The homeless cry out for shelter, and we are too busy painting the walls to the new church extension. The hungry cry out for food, and we are too busy attending conferences on reaching the lost. The poor cry out for money, and we are too busy overloading our credit limits. The young cry out for friendship, and we are too busy moralizing about how different we were at that age. The outcast cries out for acceptance, and we are too busy debating the theology of their lifestyle.

Being busy is one thing. Being busy with kingdom stuff is another. One is the lukewarm life of empty religion. The other is nothing short of Christian fanaticism. Which one are you?

Continental

I wonder what God would say to the church in Essex or Edinburgh or East Anglia today?
I wonder what God would say to you and me today?
I wonder what God would say?
I wonder …?

Coffee

'If you have ears, listen to what the Spirit says' (v. 22). So, listen up or lose out!

Orange Juice
And because of Christ, all of us can come to the Father by the same Spirit.

(EPHESIANS 2:18)

A BACKSTAGE PASS

The Big Breakfast
Don't tell anyone, but I was once involved in an event at the Royal Albert Hall in London with none other than supersinger Cliff Richard himself. Embarrassing, isn't it? Seeing the way he was mobbed by fans old and young made me think he had put in an application to be the next pope!

Security was very tight, just like Sir Cliff's leather trousers in fact. (I'm convinced that the only way he could have got those on was with a warm spoon!) Nobody could get access to the great man unless, like me, they had a little pass around their necks with the words ACCESS ALL AREAS. It meant I could look in the royal box, wander around backstage, sit in the green room, stand on the stage, and even rummage around Cliff's underwear drawer. (The latter option I declined on account of the fact that there are some things better kept a mystery in life.) I could have sold that pass for thousands to some of those Cliff fans.

The apostle Paul desperately wanted the Ephesian Christians to know that they had access to all areas – a backstage pass to the Father, authorized by Jesus Christ himself. Now they could sit with royalty, enjoy heavenly hospitality and co-star with his Son in life's unfolding drama.

Continental
We make appointments to see doctors. We schedule time to meet with work colleagues or clients. We are summoned to see teachers or judges. Yet we are invited to rush headlong into our Father's arms 24 hours a day, seven days a week.

Coffee
'Christ now gives us courage and confidence, so that we can come to God by faith' (Ephesians 3:12). That's freedom to tell him anything – he's never shocked. And confidence to know he won't judge – his Son has already taken the blame.

Orange Juice
The LORD is good! His love and faithfulness will last for ever.

(PSALM 100:5)

STOP PADDLING AROUND

The Big Breakfast
I took my two boys swimming today. But this was no ordinary swimming pool: it was called a subtropical paradise. This meant you did very little swimming and a great deal of sliding down tubes, negotiating white water rapids and squeezing into hot jacuzzi pools with oversized women in undersized costumes. The highlight for Matthew and Nathan was the regular Tarzan call and flashing lights which heralded the onset of the wave machine. We held on for dear life as the waves pounded us against the fake subtropical rocks. By the end of the session, I felt thoroughly worn out and slightly eroded at the edges.

The Psalmist reminds us that God's pounding love for us isn't like some rogue wave that wanders gently up the beach every few days and then slinks back out to sea. It's forceful, it's enduring, it's incessant, it never gives up, and it erodes away the rock-hard hearts we harbour deep within.

Maybe it's been a while since you went out into the deeper waters of God's goodness. Steal some precious time now. Other stuff can wait – it must wait. Let your soul swim. Let the power and majesty of that long-lasting love crash into your consciousness again this day.

Continental
I worshipped recently in an ancient church building over 600 years old. We sang songs and read words about the enduring love of God, from centuries past, words repeated by generations of followers. We have a great heritage to our faith because we have a God who endures for ever. You are part of something that will go on and on.

Coffee
When you watch a gripping TV drama, it often concludes with the caption: 'To be continued …' The faithfulness of our God is like that; it is 'to be continued' in your generation. Don't miss the next enthralling instalment.

Orange Juice

These are the numbers of the men armed for battle … men of Issachar, who understood the times and knew what Israel should do – 200.

(1 CHRONICLES 12:23, 32 NIV)

CONNECT WITH YOUR CULTURE

The Big Breakfast

As King David selected his 'mighty men' to rule over Israel he included, among his soldiers and brave warriors, 200 futurologists who knew the trends and how the people should respond to them.

I met a man recently who is paid by nations and huge multi-national companies to live in the year 2010. They want to know what is happening and how to shape their organizations accordingly. He holds virtual conferences, advises virtual companies on future patterns of life and work and is paid a virtual fortune for doing so!

Unless the Church learns to connect with our culture we will continue to answer yesterday's questions. If we are to regain the role of 'prophet to the nation', we need to be like the men of Issachar 'who understand the times'. For you it may mean listening to pop music instead of Christian radio occasionally. It may mean buying a daily newspaper, getting involved in local political issues. Are you wrestling with the daily dilemma of connecting with our culture while not getting contaminated by it? Where have you got into a ghetto and where have you compromised your convictions? This is a bloody battle, and none of us is exempt from the front-line.

Continental

I often get asked how we can make Jesus relevant to our culture. I always say we can't. Jesus has always been relevant to our world. It's just that the Church has cleverly disguised a contemporary Christ in organized religion.

Coffee

One eminent church leader of old said, 'The true Christian holds the Bible in one hand, a newspaper in the other and applies them both simultaneously.' So grab hold of your broadsheet and your Bible today and put them both into action.

Orange Juice

Jacob woke up suddenly and thought, 'The LORD is in this place and I didn't even know it.'

(GENESIS 28:16)

A NEW FRAGRANCE

The Big Breakfast

Debbie is the best nurse I have ever been to bed with. Well … she's the only nurse I have ever been to bed with, and she is my wife. It makes that opening line much less attention-grabbing.

Before we were married, she trained at the hospital for sick children in London. She loved her four years of training, apart from a three-month stint in a psychiatric hospital outside London. The shifts were long, and the pain-filled patients often frightening and abusive. Her small room was more like a cell. It had bars at the only window, and that looked out on to just a brick wall opposite.

On one particular occasion, the whole experience nearly broke Debbie. She had gone beyond tears of loneliness and began thinking it was time to quit. Nothing I could say or pray seemed to help, so I brought her a bunch of yellow flowers. She came off a late shift that night and the sweet smell arrested her gloom and the bright yellow colour lit up her face. She almost heard the warm sound of the Father's voice saying, 'You are my fragrance in this stale place, it's you that I choose to bring my colour into these grey tormented minds.' Surely the Lord was in this place and she had not been aware of it.

Continental

As Jacob woke up he got a new perspective on his circumstances: 'This is a fearsome place! It must be the house of God and the ladder to of heaven' (v. 17). What a great way to kick-start your mind at the beginning of another day.

Coffee

Is your work a torment to you? Does your world seem caged in and colourless? Maybe you need to wake up. To look again today and see the evidence of God's profound beauty in the most simple of ways.

Orange Juice
Your breasts are perfect; they are twin deer feeding among lilies.

(SONG OF SONGS 4:5)

GOD INVENTED SEX

The Big Breakfast
I asked one of the lads in our church youth group what his favourite Bible verse was, and he came up with this one from Song of Songs. Being a minister, I obviously discounted it immediately. But to tell you the truth, that bothered me. If it's in the Bible, why shouldn't I use it? Then I walked past a graffiti poem on a station wall:

Sex is evil
Evil is sin
Sin is forgiven
So get stuck in!

It must have been sprayed by someone with a dodgy church history. Look at the religious language they use. But where did they ever get the idea that God was anti sex? Didn't he create it in the first place? Jesus was a sexual being. He was tempted in every way and yet he never sinned. Sex is not evil. I remember from my biology class at school that the sex life of a newt involved the male depositing a sack of goodies on a leaf and then leaving it for the female to insert herself. Thank God today that he created you human and not amphibian, and say sorry to God for the times you have misused this great gift. And start again.

Continental
When God created sex he knew how powerful and yet how destructive it can be. So he created a strong container to put it in. He called it marriage. A place where two people leave their parents and cleave commitment to each other in the ceremony of marriage, and then, and only then, do they get down to the 'one flesh' bit (Matthew 19:5).

Coffee
Imagine writing such intimate words on a card to your beloved. Try it and you'll probably get a slap in the face. Yet it's that same outrageous intimacy that Song of Songs says our beloved God longs to share with you, his lover.

Orange Juice

Moses, the LORD's servant, was dead. So the LORD spoke unto Joshua, the son of Nun, who had been the assistant of Moses. The LORD said: 'My servant Moses is dead.'

(JOSHUA 1:1–2)

THE PAST IS PAST

The Big Breakfast (the prologue)

Stating the obvious or what! Of course Joshua knew that his boss had died. After all, the Israelites had been mourning his death for thirty days (Deuteronomy 34:8). So why did God feel it necessary to tell him what he already knew? It was to bury the past, once and for all, and to begin a brand new chapter in Joshua's life story.

I spent a year working alongside the missions agency Christians in Sport some time back. My main role was the summer sports camp. My great friend Steve Conner had pioneered this amazing event, growing it to near capacity in a very short space of time. To say I was nervous taking on this new task was an understatement. Steve had done such an unbeatable job, and I didn't want to let him down. I remember sitting in a hotel lobby in Cambridge, sharing my anxiety with a good friend. He ordered us both another cappuccino, pulled his Bible out of his briefcase and turned to this verse. I realized again that no matter how successful the past was, it was the past. I sense that, for many of us, our pasts are still hampering our futures. It's time to let go, to hold a funeral service for the days that are gone and to christen a new dawn, a new tomorrow.

Continental

'We have trained men to think of the future as a promised land which favoured heroes attain – not as something which everyone reaches at the rate of sixty minutes an hour, whatever he does, whoever he is' (C.S. Lewis, *The Screwtape Letters*).

Coffee

God's promise to Joshua and to you gives fresh motivation to a weary soul: 'I'll always be with you and help you as I helped Moses, and no one will ever be able to defeat you … so be strong and brave' (Joshua 1:5–6).

Orange Juice

Their leaders went through the camp, shouting, 'When you see some of the priests carrying the sacred chest, you'll know it is time to … follow the chest … Make yourself acceptable to worship the LORD, because he is going to do amazing things for us.'

(JOSHUA 3:3–5)

STOP HIDING

The Big Breakfast (Act 1)

A high-ranking officer enters to find a nervous private cleaning his rifle.

OFFICER: Come here, soldier. Here are your new orders. (He pulls an official-looking piece of paper from his tunic). When you and your division see the big G and his army on the move, come out from your safe areas and follow. Otherwise you will get left behind – or worse, get lost in the woods. This is a new order and supersedes all other orders, as we have not been this way before. End message.
PRIVATE: Right, sir … yes, sir. I will be on the lookout, sir.
OFFICER: (pauses) A word in your 'shell like', my boy.
(He glances around surreptitiously then speaks in a quiet voice.)
Clean yourself up because the word in the officer's mess is that tomorrow the big G is planning to do some amazing things!

Newly appointed Joshua was about to take his people into the Promised Land. But first they were to consecrate themselves. Which meant to wash, both inside and out. As you follow God into today's battles, take time to get clean. As you step into the shower, let the torrent of God's forgiveness overwhelm you. Now watch as God does 'amazing things for us'.

Continental

These officers insisted on vigilance because 'you've never been there before, and you won't know the way' (v. 4). Do you seem always to tread the same paths spiritually? Are you feeling stale in your devotion? Ask God to lead you along new paths so that you can find wonder again and say, 'I've never been this way before.'

Coffee

Maybe the 'amazing things' of our faith always seem to happen to others because we are not willing to leave our current positions, get cleaned up and become authentic followers.

Orange Juice

Afterwards, Jacob went back and spent the rest of the night alone. A man (God himself as Jacob eventually realized) came and fought with Jacob until just before daybreak.

(GENESIS 32:24)

GOD PICKS A FIGHT

The Big Breakfast

I've had a few nights like that. It is often in those 'alone times' that we fight in our inner selves and try to pin God to the canvas on an issue. I guess it's also in those 'alone times' when God finally has our full attention and picks a character-building fight with us in order to toughen us for the journey ahead.

I once spent three hours locked alone in my parents' porch. Although I missed an important meeting with some church leaders, I ended up with an unscheduled appointment with the Almighty himself.

I wrestled with a God who let me miss such a strategic meeting. But God fought back. He wrestled with me because my daily diary had become more important than my daily devotion, and it had been so long since I had been in the company of the King. It wasn't long before the spirit of God had turned my temporary prison into a temple of worship and I had become a hostage of a holy God instead of a slave to a gruelling schedule. Where is God getting tough with you right now? What are the issues that bring you to blows with him? Or have you given up the fight, stepped out of the ring and taken an early shower?

Continental

Jacob calls out to God mid-struggle, his arms locked around his shoulders, his voice full of gritted-teeth determination: 'You can't go until you bless me.' Now that's the kind of battle cry that would put paid to our constant whingeing.

Coffee

'Jesus, you know how I long for your gentle comfort, yet I commit myself again to your discipline and your judgement because I know you do this through the lens of love.'

Orange Juice
God cares for you, so turn all your worries over to him.

(1 PETER 5:7)

CHUCK IT ALL AT JESUS

The Big Breakfast
So what's making you anxious today? What's eating away at you deep inside? According to medical research, anxiety and worry are proven to be the root causes of a great number of physical illnesses. The effects of stress and guilt fill our hospital waiting rooms on a daily basis.

There is a great story about the author Sir Arthur Conan Doyle. As a prank, he sent a note to twelve London socialites. It simply read, 'Flee at once. All is discovered!' Within twenty-four hours they had all left the country. I guess many of us live with an undiscovered past that causes guilt to rise and worry to set in.

Whatever worry it is that has stolen sleep from you recently, the secret of finding freedom and peace is in this verse. We need to do some casting, some lobbing, some chucking, some picking it up with both hands and throwing it as hard and as far as we can. And where do we aim? At him, at Jesus, at the Prince of Peace, at the one who had no sin yet became sin for us. That's where!

Continental
'Don't fret or worry. Instead of worrying, pray. Let petitions and praises shape your worries into prayers … Before you know it, a sense of God's wholeness, everything coming together for good, will come and settle you down' (Philippians 4:6–7 *The Message*).

Coffee
What foolish follower of Christ leaves worry at heaven's door and yet continues to pick over it when the Master says, 'You're under my care now and I'm dealing with this one'? So let it go!

Orange Juice

The LORD said to Abram: 'Leave your country, your family, and your relatives and go to the land that I will show you.'

(GENESIS 12:1)

FANATICAL FAITH

The Big Breakfast

He has to be one of my all-time Bible heroes. Not so much from his list of impressive achievements but more from what he had to give up to get them. He left the whole kit and caboodle to 'go to the land that I (God) will show you'. He had no idea where he was going, only a deep sense of God calling him there.

Imagine you wake up one morning, grab a bowl of frosted E numbers and jump in the shower. As the Jojoba Haircare Mousse froths its way down your face, you hear a strange heavenly voice rise from beyond the steam: 'Leave this house. Give it to someone who really needs it. Cash in your savings plans, sell the motor and scribble a quick note to the folks. Wave farewell to work and the gang and get yourself to Heathrow Airport post haste.'

'You expect me to give up … what will the boss say? … and my folks! You can't be … where am I going anyway?'

'Don't fret, just go and I'll give you more details en route.'

Maybe it was this kind of fanatical faith that gave Abraham's picture pride of place in God's great hall of the faithful. It's stunning to see what faith like this can achieve. What have you got to walk away from to walk closer with him?

Continental

I have often heard preachers smugly expound that 'Faith is spelt R.I.S.K.' I always think, 'No it's not. It is spelt F.A.I.T.H., and anyway, what's so risky about stepping out into the centre of God's will for your life? It's actually got to be the safest place to be!'

Coffee

'Abraham had faith and obeyed God. He was told to go to the land that God had said would be his, and he left for a country he had never seen' (Hebrews 11:8). Get yourself a good faith lift today.

Orange Juice

'Abba, Father,' he said, 'everything is possible for you. Take this cup from me. Yet not what I will, but what you will.'

(MARK 14:36 NIV)

MY DADDY

The Big Breakfast

I flew from Beirut to Jordan on the day that Yasser Arafat was on the lawn of the White House signing the Middle East peace treaty with Benjamin Netanyahu. Not the best plan I have ever made. Security everywhere was tight. I sat quietly panicking in the airport's 'final departure' lounge.

The moment was broken by the cries of two little Jordanian girls who had temporarily lost their parents. With tears rolling down their cheeks, one cried for 'Imma' – Mummy – while the other sobbed 'Abba' – Daddy. At the thought of being separated from their parents, all formality went as they cried out. As Jesus wrestled with his mission in the Garden of Gethsemane, he too cried out. Not to the Almighty or to the King of Kings, but to his Daddy. I don't think it was the nails that Jesus feared the most: it was being separated from the Father he loved.

Maybe today you feel like a lost and abandoned child in a crowded world. You used to sit so safely in your Father's arms, and you long for those days again. Throw away your pride and cry out loud again for Abba to come and rediscover his child.

Continental

Don't send a memo to God requesting a meeting at his earliest convenience vis-à-vis a few hitches in your life plan. Stop and realize how intimate he wants to be with you. Start to dwell on the truth that everything is possible for him, even among the twisted branches of your Garden of Gethsemane.

Coffee

'This resurrection life you received from God is not a timid, grave-tending life. It's adventurously expectant, greeting God with a childlike "What's next, Papa?" God's spirit touches our spirit and confirms who we really are ... father and children' (Romans 8:15 *The Message*).

Orange Juice

For this reason I remind you to fan into flame the gift of God, which is in you through the laying on of my hands.

(2 TIMOTHY 1:6)

LIGHT THE FIRE AGAIN

The Big Breakfast

Last night was a cold, wintry evening as we sat with friends around a roaring log fire. As the evening went on the fire cooled. Where there had once been a blaze of searing heat there now remained only a grate of charred ashes. However, somebody noticed the problem, quickly picked up a poker and began vigorously prodding and poking the dying embers. As if from nowhere, the fire found new energy and began to blaze again, warming our cold toes and doing the job it was designed to do.

Do you remember the time when your soul burned with a passion to achieve great things for the kingdom of God? What put that fire out?

Recently I sat chatting to a 35-year-old man whose dreams from his youth had now grown cold. 'I had such big plans,' he said, as he told me the story of how he had been prayed for by his church and was planning an inner-city outreach project. 'I got married, had kids, and got this job offer with a huge salary and company BMW. I just can't seem to find a way back. My passion is dying. I feel like I've lost my dreams.'

If you are going 'to fan into flame the gift of God that is in you' it may take some vigorous prodding and poking to start the fire blazing once more. Don't let it grow cold.

Continental

The philosopher Soren Kierkegaard once said, 'Life must be understood backwards; but … it must be lived forwards.' Look back to those dreams of old and fan them into flame once more.

Coffee

Don't start blaming everyone else for stealing your gifts and your passion away. Paul's reminder to Timothy was for him to do the fanning. It's your responsibility.

Orange Juice

We must try to become mature and start thinking about more than just the basic things we were taught about Christ.

(HEBREWS 6:1)

MOVING ON

The Big Breakfast

I love the story about the young girl who falls out of bed one night with a great thud. Mum and Dad rush upstairs to find her sitting up in a daze, rubbing her head. 'What happened?' Mum asks. 'I think I stayed too close to where I got in,' she replies.

Maturity in Christ means not staying too close to where we got in. It means moving on in all walks of life. My younger son is moving on from mashed-up soft stuff to proper cereals. My next lad is moving on from nursery to big school. My wife is moving on from attending a small group to leading a small group. I am moving on from just typing sermons to learning PowerPoint presentations. Our church is moving on from news-sheets to web pages. Even my mother-in-law is moving on from landlines to mobiles. We all need to move on or we will stand still.

If my kids stayed with porridge and pre-school they would never grow. If Debbie and I stayed with the tried and tested ways of working we would never develop. If the Church sticks with yesterday's communication methods it will never be heard.

Don't go back over the old lessons you learnt about Jesus. Go on to grown-up teaching.

Continental

Peter the Great, who was once the Tsar of Russia, said, 'I have conquered an empire but I have not been able to conquer myself.' We need to make that inner journey if we are ever to grow up in Christ.

Coffee

The CEO of General Motors once told a group of employees, 'Sometimes it's not incremental changes we need, but to go out on the lunatic fringe!' What fringe do you need to step out on to today in order to kick-start your 'growing up' in Christ?

Orange Juice
This is what I say to all who will listen to me: Love your enemies, and be good to everyone who hates you. Ask God to bless anyone who curses you, and pray for everyone who is cruel to you. *(LUKE 6:27–8)*

BEAT THE GRUDGE

The Big Breakfast
Get the bigger picture with this one, please. The verse doesn't tell us to walk away from those who hate us or treat us badly. There is no sense of mere tolerance here. We are clearly commanded to do them good, to offer them a blessing and to pray for them.

I knew a man who disliked me so much that he twisted the truth about me publicly, spread damaging rumours about my character privately and told my closest friends that they should abandon me. Everything within me wanted to hurt him. Everything within God wanted me to love him, to bless him and even to pray for him. If it hadn't been for the advice of a wise friend, I might well have gone with my emotions and missed the adventure of going against the grain.

I began by reluctantly praying God's very best for him. That's where my attitude slowly started to change. I vowed never to speak badly of him publicly, and made every effort to talk well of him in private. I even sent him a gift as a blessing.

I discovered that real freedom would never come from revenge, but only from real love. I also discovered that I could never have behaved that way but for the love of good friends and the grace of a great God.

Continental
Winston Churchill once remarked that we should listen to our friends *and* our enemies, as they are both telling us the truth from a slightly different perspective. When the rocks of criticism fly, we must learn not to build a wall with them but to use them to build a solid foundation for our character.

Coffee
'This is what I say to all who will listen to me.' Don't go deaf on God; instead, deal with whatever issue it is today, before your head hits the pillow.

Orange Juice

Don't destroy yourself by getting drunk, but let the Spirit fill your life.

(EPHESIANS 5:18)

GET DRUNK!

The Big Breakfast

My initial years as a Christian were spent with believers whose passion for God was only surpassed by their disdain for 'the Devil's urine'. I remember one older gentleman explaining away the apostle Paul's advice for Timothy to 'take a little wine to help his stomach trouble' as meaning he should rub it on (1 Timothy 5:23)! I was often sternly reminded about the first part of this verse, which in itself is excellent advice – 'Don't destroy yourself by getting drunk'. It was only in latter years that I grasped the importance of the 'but let the Spirit fill your life' bit. Is Paul suggesting that the infilling of God's Spirit is akin to having a skinful of best Beaujolais? In some ways, yes.

Wine makes people lose their inhibitions, it makes them dance like constipated octopuses and not bother about what anyone else thinks. It frees their emotions to express inner feelings. Being filled with the rich wine of God's Spirit gives freedom to worship, to embrace the passion of our love affair with Jesus. He enables us to express our affection for each other with genuine honesty and vulnerability. Pay a visit to heaven's vineyard today and swap the headache of too much booze for the heartbeat of the Father's best vintage.

Continental

Nancy Astor wrote in the *Christian Herald* back in 1960, 'The only reason I don't drink is because I wish to know when I am having a good time.' Do your fun times rely on a glass in your hand? Can you still laugh and play without the drug of drink? What spirit are you addicted to?

Coffee

'Wine makes you mean, beer makes you quarrelsome – a staggering drunk is not much fun' (Proverbs 20:1 *The Message*). How easy would it be for you to fast from alcohol for a month? I'm serious.

Orange Juice

Jesus asked a third time, 'Simon ... do you love me?' Peter was hurt because Jesus had asked him three times ... he told Jesus, 'Lord, you know everything. You know I love you.'

(JOHN 21:17)

DO YOU LOVE ME?

The Big Breakfast

We are quite limited when we use the word 'love' in the English language. We have to use the same word to say, 'I think I love you, Doris,' as we would use to say, 'I'd love a bag of chips.' The ancient Greeks were far more expressive:

Phileo love was the love of things or friends.
Agape love was unconditional love – the kind of love God has for his children.

After the resurrected Jesus has finished his breakfast with Peter, he asks him three times, 'Peter, do you love me?' The first couple of times Jesus asks, 'Peter, do you *agape* me – love me unconditionally?' Yet both times Peter answers, 'Lord, you know that I *phileo* you – love you as a friend.' Eventually Jesus asks a final time, but this time he says, 'Peter, do you *phileo* me?' 'Yes, Lord,' Peter replies. 'You know that I *phileo* you.'

Was Jesus dropping his standard? Letting Peter off the hook? I don't think so. I'm convinced that he was saying to Peter, 'You know the kind of love I long for from you, but let's start from where you are.' God longs for our exclusive attention today, yet he begins with our faltering affection.

Continental

Before Jesus was crucified, Peter told him he would die for him. What happened? He ended up denying Jesus three times. It's this same Peter that Jesus reinstates and of whom Jesus says, 'I will build my Church on you.' Gives us all hope, eh?

Coffee

Jesus doesn't run through a 'why did you deny me three times?' debate with Peter. He simply asks, 'Do you love me ... I mean really love me?' How would you respond to that same question asked of you today?

Orange Juice

Jesus looked at his disciples and said: 'God will bless you people who are poor. His kingdom belongs to you!'

(LUKE 6:20)

HOW POOR DO YOU HAVE TO BE?

The Big Breakfast

What kind of a deal is that? The kingdom of heaven is yours if you are poor? I mean, how poor do you have to be in order to qualify for this 'once-in-a-lifetime-never-to-be-repeated' offer? Is Jesus talking about the poverty of a student living in bedsit land with no grant, a huge debt and only the smell of last night's curry for breakfast? Or is it the poverty of the bag lady who pushes her life in a shopping trolley from doorway to doorway? Or maybe he means the heartbreaking poverty of the starving African child or the homeless Kosovan refugee?

I struggled with this verse for so long until I sat over a fairly traded decaffeinated coffee with a friend of mine who has travelled to some of the world's nations with Tearfund. 'So how poor do you have to be, Dave?' His answer was swift, and one he had made a thousand times before in as many such meetings. He simply amplified the verse for me: 'Blessed are you who have seen everything the world has to give and realize that the most it has to give is poverty.' He repeated it, then talked some more.

I nodded in the appropriate pauses, but I listened to none of it. Something had happened deep in my soul – I had understood. Do you, too?

Continental

The phone rang as I wrote this piece today. It was a man who has walked out on his faith, his job, his home and his friends for a woman he loves but can never have. Now he wants to taste God's kingdom again. I read him this verse from *The Message*: 'You're blessed when you've lost it all. God's kingdom is there for the finding.'

Coffee

When you wake up to the fact that there is something better in life than money or sex, fame or power, then – and only then – is the kingdom of God truly yours!

Orange Juice

Whoever claims to live in him must walk as Jesus did.

(1 JOHN 2:6 NIV)

EXCHANGE YOUR NIKES

The Big Breakfast

If you sing the songs on a Sunday you've got to walk to his tune on a Monday. Hypocrisy stinks. Jesus had some strong words to say to hypocrites. He used the kind of language that wouldn't get him invited back to preach in their churches. But frankly, he didn't care about that. It's amazing how gentle and graceful Jesus was with adulterers and swindlers, yet how righteously rude he was to the religious rulers.

The question that often haunts me as a Christ follower, a parent, a husband and a leader is this: can God trust me? Am I a responsible ambassador? Do I love as Jesus loved, care as Jesus cared and walk where Jesus walked? 'Whoever claims to live in him must walk as Jesus did.' I so often stake the claim, yet so rarely walk the walk.

He walked tall – proud of his heritage. He walked far – going the extra mile. He walked humbly – not with the rich but the poor. But what I love about him most is that he walked *his* way – never sticking to the prescribed paths.

Yesterday I met a friend I hadn't seen for years. We hugged evangelically (one foot on the ground). Then he asked pointedly, 'How is your walk?' Hum … good question …

Continental

Go on … 1 to 10 … how is your walk? A strong 10, a mediocre 5 or a flagging 1? Or have you gone the whole hog and turned 'March for Jesus' into 'Sit Still for Jesus'? Maybe today you need to exchange your Nikes for his sandals. Spend the day in his shoes – you'll find they fit better than you think.

Coffee

When C.S. Lewis was asked for his views on hypocrisy he answered, 'How difficult it is to avoid having a special standard for oneself!' How self-revealing are you? Could you share your inconsistencies with a friend and begin to deal with them?

Orange Juice

Instead, they were longing for a better country.

(HEBREWS 11:16 NIV)

A BETTER PLACE TO LIVE

The Big Breakfast

Russian comedian Yakov Smirnoff writes, 'Coming from the Soviet Union I was not prepared… On my first shopping trip I saw powdered milk – you just add water and you get milk. Then I saw powdered orange juice – you just add water and you get orange juice. Then I saw baby powder and I thought to myself, wow – what a wonderful country!'

These few words from Hebrews ignite again a soul-wrenching longing for a better nation than the one we have now.

A country where locksmiths go out of business because stealing doesn't exist.
A country where divorce courts remain empty because couples remain faithful.
A country where maximum security becomes minimum occupancy because killing stops.
And a country where my team always wins the league.

Michael Jackson's 'Man in the Mirror' was right. 'If you want to make the world a better place take a look at yourself and make a change.' It's the only way to see the dream become

Continental

A little lad was throwing washed-up starfish back into the Mediterranean Sea. An intrigued tourist asked how he intended to make a difference to so many. The boy simply picked up another, tossed it back into the cool water and said, 'I made a difference to that one, didn't I?' Start small, but make sure you start!

Coffee

You might not be able to change everybody's world everywhere, but you can change somebody's world somewhere. Whose world do you want to make a change in today? Go do it!

Orange Juice
Greet one another with a holy kiss.

(ROMANS 16:16 NIV)

KISSING WITH CONFIDENCE

The Big Breakfast

You now have my full permission to kiss in church. Unless, of course, the person in the pew next to you was the winner of last year's Mr Halitosis competition. The early Church practised it as part of their regular worship; maybe that's why their services went with such a swing! The New Testament condones it (1 Peter 5:14; 1 Corinthians 16:20). So why has our Western 'middle-classness' robbed us of the experience? The Living Bible reduces this verse to 'shake hands warmly with each other'. And *The Message* is not much better: it reads 'holy embraces all round'. What's wrong with a holy kiss? As long as we understand the difference between a holy kiss and an unholy kiss to be around 3 minutes, we should be all right.

When I first visited an Arab country I was staggered to see men holding hands in public. I was even more taken aback when they greeted me with a full-blown smacker right on the lips! It seems to me that many of us men have lost the intimacy of same-sex relationships because of the fear of confused sexuality. Can we ever learn again to go beyond the handshake, and embrace? Can we ever grow close enough in our relationships to take our greetings beyond the verbal?

Continental

Sharing a holy kiss would be guaranteed to spice up the dullest of church services and serve to remind us again that meeting together doesn't make us church. We meet together and we share the intimacies of our lives together because we are church!

Coffee
'Love one another. In the same way I loved you, you love one another. This is how everyone will recognise that you are my disciples' John 13:35 (*The Message*).

Orange Juice
Get ready for war! Be eager to fight. Line up for battle and prepare to attack.

(JOEL 3:9)

TAKE THE KING'S SHILLING

The Big Breakfast
We must get away from the idea that Church is a Sunday-school picnic complete with fondant fancies and warm lemonade. We must recapture the image of a small mud-splattered army who meet together each week for the commanding office to heal our battle scars, lead our war cry and roll out the strategy for the coming offensive.

We must lose the image of the Church as a convalescent home for retired or just tired soldiers. We only retreat in order to prepare again for advance. God doesn't have a divine, MASH-like helicopter that rescues us from life's battles and drops us back in the warmth of the officers' mess. If he did have such a helicopter he would drop the winch and on the end of it would be Jesus himself, who promises to walk through the battlefield with us.

Until late in the nineteenth century, the British army recruited men by giving them the King's Shilling. That coin would have been a small fortune to those men, and taking it meant they were officially conscripted – no backing out. Many fought in bloody wars. Many lost their lives.

Hear the cry again this day – 'Get ready for war!' Gladly accept the King's Shilling as a sign of your commitment to the cause.

Continental
We live in enemy-occupied territory. Our forces are outnumbered and out-resourced. Yet when the Spirit of God fell on 120 followers in that upper room, all heaven broke out and all hell ran scared as together they turned the known world upside down. The devil may seem a mighty foe, but our God is the almighty champion.

Coffee
C.T. Studd once said, 'I don't want to live within the sound of chapel bell, I want to run a rescue shop within a yard of hell.' Where are your priorities?

Orange Juice

Then Peter stood up with the Eleven, raised his voice and addressed the crowd: 'Fellow Jews and all of you who live in Jerusalem, *let me explain this to you.*'

(ACTS 2:14 NIV)

LET ME EXPLAIN

The Big Breakfast

As a preacher, I spend most of my time *proclaiming* the story of God: in schools, at Alpha, on the streets and in people's homes. But not Peter. He spent his time *explaining*. God had spoken quite well for himself by all the miraculous things he had done previously. Peter merely said, 'Let me explain them to you.' To be honest, I'm getting fed up with all this proclamation. I want to do some explanation.

You're well again despite the prognosis – let me explain …
You've found a job when they said you never would – let me explain …
You've found a partner when they said you were still on the shelf – let me explain …
You feel a peace you can't understand, you've lost that bitterness deep within, you can forgive now after all these years and you don't know why? Let me explain …

Let the work of God in your life speak for itself today. Then hear yourself repeating Peter's words – 'let me explain'.

Continental

It's not often our words about God that demand any explanation from our friends. It's more likely to be things such as spending some time with the office outcast, being honest on this month's expenses claim or choosing to see the best rather than fuel the rumour. Does your life provoke that kind of explanation?

Coffee

There should be things in our daily lives that can be explained only by God. Reflect on those things in your life.

Orange Juice
People who try to save their lives will lose them, and those who lose their lives will save them.

(LUKE 17:33)

PROTECT LIFE OR PURSUE IT?

The Big Breakfast
One commentator said that no other saying of Jesus is given such emphasis in the gospels as this one. This is a big thing to grasp. Jesus tells his followers that there are two ways to look at life: keep it or let it go; protect it or pursue it.

As you walk life's road you will inevitably come to Decision Junction. The rickety signpost points left towards 'Cosy Town – via Pipe and Slippers Lane'. The road is busy and well lit this way, with flashing neon signs advertising take-it-easy restaurants and don't-get-too-involved family fun parks. The sign also points right towards 'Adrenaline City – via Adventure Boulevard'. The road here is a steep climb, and not many choose to take it. However, the rumour is that it's a long haul to the top but, boy, is the view worth it!

So which road will you take today? The safe route that says if I don't take part they won't criticize me? Or the adventurous route where the adrenaline rush of active involvement pulsates constantly through your veins?

You see, whichever route you choose you'll arrive in heaven. But choose the wrong route and you'll have no stories to tell when you get to your destination.

Continental
Imagine if Jesus had chosen to protect his life rather than vigorously pursing it. Safeguarding his reputation would have kept him away from prostitutes, the poor and the pious. Safeguarding his life would have kept him away from criminals, critics and ultimately the cross.

Coffee
'If you grasp and cling to life on your terms, you'll lose it, but if you let that life go, you'll get life on God's terms' (*The Message*). Decide what you need to let go of today.

Orange Juice

They said to each other, 'This isn't right. Today is a day to celebrate, and we haven't told anyone else what has happened.'

(2 KINGS 7:9)

THE BEST-KEPT SECRET

The Big Breakfast

It would have taken a whole herd of wild horses to drag me away from the delivery room the day my first son was born. Eventually, the midwife put Matthew into my arms and I couldn't take my eyes off him. So cute and cuddly, so perfectly formed, so handsome, so much like his dad!

I was forced to pass him back to the nurse to get him cleaned up and dressed. Debbie looked at me with one of those 'isn't-there-something-you-ought-to-be-doing?' stares. I had clean forgotten. This was the best news the family had ever had and we were keeping it to ourselves. There were parents to tell, friends to inform and a church keen to hear.

If only we could re-imagine the enormity of our new birth in Christ we would be rushing to the phone, fax or email systems at our disposal to tell the world the good news. But we seem to have lost the sense of urgency. I spoke to a good friend yesterday who was giving the remainder of his ministry to turning his church from maintenance to mission. It wasn't easy, and some had left. His concluding comment was, 'Life's too short to waste it on church politics when there's a world hungry for our news.'

Continental

I once heard a brilliant seminar on evangelism. The whole session took only two minutes and consisted of just one sentence. It was the most freeing and profound teaching I had ever heard on the subject. Here is the entire seminar for you, free of charge: 'Find out what you really enjoy doing and go and do it with the unchurched.'

Coffee

C.S. Lewis said, 'God used an ass to convert a prophet; perhaps if we do our poor best we shall be allowed a stall near it in the celestial stable.' Don't buy the lie – God will even use donkeys like you and me!

Orange Juice

When you … do anything … always do it to honour God.

(1 CORINTHIANS 10:31)

TOTAL DEDICATION

The Big Breakfast

I love this verse. Total dedication to the cause. A cry to go above and beyond the call of duty. Billy Graham once received a letter from a communist who was breaking up with his girlfriend. It oozes with infectious dedication:

We communists do not have the time or the money for many movies, or concerts, or T-bone steaks, or decent homes, or new cars. We have been described as fanatics. We are fanatics. We have a cause to fight for and a definite purpose in life… There is one thing which I am in dead earnest about, and that is the communist cause. It is my life, my business, my religion, my hobby, my sweetheart, my wife, my mistress and my bread and meat. I work at it in the daytime and dream of it at night… I cannot carry on a friendship, a love affair or even a conversation without relating it to this force which both drives and guides my life… I've already been in jail because of my ideals, and if necessary, I'm ready to go before a firing squad.

This kind of fighting talk stirs the heart again to dedication, especially if we were to live our lives for Christ as this communist did for his cause! Don't lose the sense of passion that has exploded in your soul today.

Continental

'Let us not rust out. Let us not glide through the world then slip quietly out without having blown the trumpet loud and long for our blessed redeemer. At the very least let us see to it that the Devil holds a thanksgiving party in Hell when he gets the news of our departure from the field of battle' (C.T. Studd).

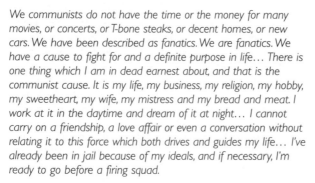

Coffee

'God, hear my prayer. I want you to know that whatever I do this day, I do it for your glory. Because I know that whatever you do this day, you do it for my best.'

Orange Juice

The harvest is past, the summer is gone, and we are not saved.

(JEREMIAH 8:20 NIV)

THE SADDEST OF VERSES

The Big Breakfast

I think this is the saddest verse in the entire Bible. 'Harvest past' – it's like turning up for a party, liberally splashed with half a bottle of CK One, with all your best pulling clobber on, and everybody's gone. The party happened and you missed it.

'Summer gone' – it's like going off on a sunshine holiday with your factor 25 in one hand and your paperback thriller in the other, only to discover the hotel closed, the sky clouding over and the locals cleaning up.

'Salvation missed' – it's like watching a sky full of shooting stars, standing slightly scared by the ocean's edge on a blustery day, or watching a baby being born, and thinking, 'Maybe there is a God in heaven ... ah, but what the heck.'

'The harvest is past, the summer is gone, and we are not saved' – it's all too late. Why didn't I do something about it before?

I read this to a friend who's not a Christian. 'That's me!' he said, in a surprised tone of voice, 'I've often looked at the world around and the intricacies of the human body and wondered if God really did exist. But I always banished the thought from my mind as stupid.'

Continental

Arthur Koestler, who wrote the classic *The Ghost in the Machine*, once bleakly commented, 'God seems to have left the receiver off the hook, and time is running out.' The truth is that God came in person to planet earth two thousand years ago with a rescue plan. If time is running out, it's our problem.

Coffee

'That time has come. Now is the day for you to be saved' (2 Corinthians 6:2). Put it off no more.

Orange Juice
If you won't help the poor, don't expect to be heard when you cry out for help.

(PROVERBS 21:13)

THE NOT-SO-SECRET DIARY

The Big Breakfast
The Not-So-Secret Diary of a Frustrated Christian (aged 35 and a bit)

Sunday
Decided to walk home from church. Why is it you never hear church people say, 'Oi! It's my turn to sit on the front row this morning'? Preached about prayer. Why is it you never hear people say, 'I was so enthralled with your talk that I never noticed you went twenty minutes over time'?

Monday
Wanted to start the week in prayer. Ended up trawling through endless third-world charity letters. Chucked the lot.

Tuesday
Day off. Decided to also have a day off from praying and go and spend some money on myself.

Wednesday
Got bothered by the *Big Issue** salesman, along with a bloke on a blanket with his dog. Took sanctuary in a teashop. Thought I could pray there. Read the paper instead.

*A magazine sold on the streets by the homeless.

Continental
If we don't listen to the poor in our world, God in heaven says he won't listen to you and me when we pray. Is that why your prayer life seems so rusty? Is that why answers seem so few and far between?

Coffee
Jim Wallis said, 'Many Christians gladly get converted from their sin but never get converted to the poor.' Begin that process today. At the very least, buy a copy of *The Big Issue* or check out its website (www.bigissue.com).

Orange Juice

Around midday the sky turned dark and stayed that way until the middle of the afternoon. The sun stopped shining.

(LUKE 23:44)

WHO GETS THE BLAME?

The Big Breakfast

I remember the eerie feeling of watching the midday sky turn cold and dark during a recent total eclipse. But what happened in the three hours of darkness when the carpenter from Nazareth ended his days on a torturous wooden cross?

God was apportioning the blame. He blamed his own Son, his own spotless lamb, who had never committed a crime in his life; never done anything wrong.

He blamed him for the twisted crime of the paedophile.

He blamed him for the dark heart of the terrorist.

He blamed him for the murderous mind of the serial killer.

He pointed the finger of blame at his own Son for every wrong thought that has ever tempted you into sinful action.

In those dreadful hours of darkness when the sun stopped shining, the God of heaven lifted the burden of guilt from your shoulders and loaded them on to the Son he loved. Then he sent him to hell in your place. Worship God today. Even if it means getting in late, stop and hold an audience with a God whose love for you goes beyond your wildest imaginings. And say thank you … thank you … thank you.

Continental

I meet many people who blame God for the pain in their lives. They blame him for the death of a loved one, for the handicapped child or the raw deal of a partner's fury. The truth is, they are two thousand years too late. God has already blamed Jesus for all the sin that causes all the pain in all our lives.

Coffee

Eventually Jesus cried out, 'Father, I put myself in your hands!' (Luke 23:46). 'Dad! I'm coming home!' He went home to prepare a place for you (John 14:2). Let the hope of that homecoming crack a smile today.

Orange Juice
I'm completely worn out; my time has been wasted.

(ISAIAH 49:4)

CLEAR VISION

The Big Breakfast
Why does so much of what we do in life feel like hard work but with very little purpose? I think it's because we so often lose our focus. The end goal has gone fuzzy on the horizon. I went to Disneyland a few years back. If you ask the ticket-collectors, road-sweepers or entertainers what their role is, the answer is always the same: 'To make people happy who come to Disneyland.' They have a clear goal, and it works.

In 1789 William Wilberforce came before the British parliament to plea for an end to slavery. Twenty years later, just days after his death, his life's vision became reality.

In 1907 Henry Ford told the world that he was going to make cars affordable for the average man. The world sniggered, but a decade later millions of Model T Fords rolled off the production line at just $290 each.

The sheer power of a clear vision. It ignites passion in the soul and makes dreams come true. A lack of vision will always lead to frustration. Do you know why you do what you do? Is it clearly stated? For one famous hospital in London it's 'Child first and always'; for our church it's 'Helping people to make life work'. What is it for your life, your church, or your workplace?

Continental
Bill Hybels says, 'Vision is a picture of the future that creates a passion in you.' Have you got the kind of dream where nothing will stop you fulfilling it – not money, not reputation, not nothing!

Coffee
Charles Swindoll said, 'Vision is essential for survival … it encompasses vast vistas outside the realm of the predictable, the safe and the expected. No wonder we perish without it!'

Orange Juice

Now I'm eighty-five … I'm just as strong today as I was then, and I can still fight as well in battle. So I'm asking you for the hill country that the LORD promised me that day.

(JOSHUA 14:10–11)

HOLD ON TO THE DREAM

The Big Breakfast

What kind of an old person will you be? If you read these verses, you'll discover that this old man, Caleb, had a dream from God that he kept for forty-five years. Not even old age was going to rob him of it. So he took a risk: with his pension book in one hand and his false teeth in the other, he went for the hill country that God had promised him all those years back.

You will never get anything of value unless you hold on to a dream and then take a risk to see it happen. I reckon every bloke remembers his first kiss with a girl. I may have looked cool on the outside when I puckered up to Debbie, ready to minister to her through the laying on of lips, but inside was sheer panic. What if I missed! And I clearly remember the night I asked her to marry me. My emotions had never known such chaos. I was as nervous as a frog in a biology class. What if she said no? I took a risk and got something of great value – my dream girl. I'm only glad that God didn't do a Caleb on me and make me wait 45 years! You never get anything of value unless you take a risk.

It's interesting to note that Caleb wanted the hill country. Dreams can often be an uphill struggle, but it's there that we meet with God.

Continental

Helen Keller once interviewed a young girl who was both blind and deaf. She asked what could be worse than having those two disabilities. The girl replied, 'Having your sight but having no vision.'

Coffee

Henry Ford said, 'The poor man is not the man without a cent but a man without a dream.' If you haven't got a dream, find someone who has and let it rub off on you. If you have – go for it!

Orange Juice

First, I must see the nail scars in his hands and touch them with my finger. I must put my hand where the spear went into his side. I won't believe it unless I do this!

(JOHN 20:25)

DOUBT IS NOT WRONG

The Big Breakfast

I drove back buzzing from an incredible worship service last week. It was probably the best talk on discipleship I had ever heard. It was probably the best talk on discipleship I had ever given! Yet as I drove home through the darkness, I started to wonder if there really was a God in heaven. Are we just making all this up? Is it all no more than clever fantasy?

How could my heart jump so quickly from devotion to doubt? I turned to Thomas for solace. He wasn't there when the resurrected Jesus first appeared to the disciples. He had given up hope and run away. I find it incredible that so many of us doubters run away from the place where we will find help rather than run towards it. Thomas should have been in the upper room the first time. After all, he wasn't the only one who was afraid: the other disciples had locked themselves in there for fear of the Jews (John 20:19).

But Jesus came back a second time just for him, and said, 'Peace be with you.' One of the last recorded conversations of Jesus was with a man racked with doubt. So take heart today. Doubt isn't wrong, it isn't a sin. In fact, faith is developed as we walk through the furnace of doubt!

Continental

Then Jesus said, 'Thomas, do you have faith because you have seen me? The people who have faith in me without seeing me are the ones who are really blessed!' (John 20:29). That's us! We've not seen him, yet we believe, so that makes us the blessed ones.

Coffee

Tennyson was once quoted as saying, 'There is more faith in honest doubt, believe me, than in half the creeds!' Simply reciting the facts doesn't show faith: it just shows memory. Yes, you can doubt your faith at times, but you can also pray, 'I do have faith! Please help me to have even more.'

Orange Juice

Don't condemn others, and God won't condemn you. God will be as hard on you as you are on others! He will treat you exactly as you treat them.

(MATTHEW 7:1–2)

JUDGE AND BE JUDGED

The Big Breakfast

When I was in my early twenties I left a career in retail marketing to become an evangelist with a British missions team called Saltmine. I was very green when I started. Not long after I joined, I went to speak at a large church in London. I had got there early to set out some of my advertising material, and then took my place on the platform, watching the suited Sunday congregation slip into the service during the first song.

In the crowd I noticed a small crumpled lady dressed in a dirty raincoat held together with string. Carrying two well-worn carrier bags, she barged her way through the well-dressed worshippers and found a seat right on the front row. It was almost as if she was a regular and someone had saved her a seat there. I leant across to the minister and made some derogatory comment about 'waifs and strays' and security problems in this part of London. 'I'd be careful how you judge,' he replied. 'Edna has led more street people to Jesus than I can begin to tell you about. She doesn't have a glossy brochure to advertise her ministry and she never goes to conferences, but she's the best evangelist I know.'

Jesus was right: 'God will be as hard on you as you are on others.' It hit me square in the face!

Continental

I may have wanted the ground to swallow me up but I learnt a valuable lesson that day: 'Don't judge or you will be judged!' Put this one into practice and you will be spared the embarrassment of opening your mouth as I did and putting your foot right in it!

Coffee

The composer Sibelius said 'A statue has never been set up in honour of a critic.' Train your tongue to reduce the negative and accentuate the positive.

Orange Juice
If we claim to be in the light but hate someone, we are still in the dark.

(1 JOHN 2:9)

STOP CURSING THE DARKNESS

The Big Breakfast
I heard a story recently about a man called George Burton. George had been going to church for years, listening to the faithful complaining about the 'yobs on the street corners who frighten the old people'. He decided to offer help rather than a critical cold shoulder. He convinced the church of the need, raised the cash and eventually opened the Mayflower Centre in Canning Town, London. For the commissioning service he entitled his talk 'Better to light a candle than curse the darkness'.

The first day the centre opened, some of the local heavies came in to check the place out. They stayed long enough to shout some abuse at the workers and then broke the windows on the way out. This same scenario was played out night after night. The church people did their best to support him, but spent most of their energy asking George why he carried on with such a lost cause. Yet the Mayflower Centre persevered and became a success. George Burton went on to write a book entitled *People Matter More Than Things*.

Are you too busy cursing the darkness to light a candle; to offer a flickering hope to a lost generation?

Continental
In the 1870s there was a young man who frequently preached to the poor around London. His methods were superbly Christ-like, yet the church leaders would have nothing to do with him. Eventually, after turning his hand to painting for a while, he committed suicide. His name – Vincent Van Gogh.

Coffee
'Anyone who claims to be intimate with God ought to live the same kind of life Jesus lived' (1 John 2:6 *The Message*). Allow your hearts to burst with intimacy as your hands begin to get grubby with the business of the kingdom.

Orange Juice
'O Lord God,' I said, 'I can't do that! I'm far too young! I am only a youth.'

(JEREMIAH 1:6 LIVING BIBLE)

AGE DOESN'T MATTER

The Big Breakfast
Why do we presume that youth and inexperience should exclude us from being used by God? The disciples were young people, most of them in their teens and twenties when Jesus called them. He loved the buzz of working with young people.

In most churches you have to be older than Jesus to get on the flower rota! If I may, I would like to offer you an apology. If you are a younger person who has got the impression that you can only serve God properly if you are over 45, married and have a different voice for when you pray – then I'm sorry. It's not like that.

I can remember being told constantly that I was part of tomorrow's Church and that one day I would be able to speak or lead or sing or pray. Unless, of course, I wanted to help in the Sunday school, in which case I could begin immediately. Listen – you are part of today's Church, and don't let anyone tell you otherwise. The skill is this: don't let the 'farties' like me look down on you because you are young, but lead the way in speech, in life, in love, in faith and in purity (taken from I Timothy 4:12).

Continental
God says to the young Jeremiah, 'Don't say you're too young … I promise to be with you and keep you safe, so don't be afraid.' Be cheeky for the kingdom today and don't be afraid!

Coffee
'Nursing infants gurgle choruses about you; toddlers shout the songs that drown out enemy talk and silence atheist babble!' (Psalm 8:2 *The Message*). Hold your head up high, walk tall and walk humbly. Understand again today that your age must never stop you living out your heavenly dreams.

Orange Juice

Faith makes us sure of what we hope for and gives us proof of what we cannot see.

(HEBREWS 11:1)

WHAT IS FAITH?

The Big Breakfast

I was always under the impression that having faith was about gritting your teeth, screwing up your eyes and hoping for the best. To have enough faith to see somebody healed meant shouting your prayers louder than a soccer manager standing on the touch line with his side losing 4–0.

Faith is not about how loud you shout. It's not even about how much of it you have. It's about where you put it. Imagine you are standing by a lake frozen over with a paper-thin layer of cracked ice. You may have so much faith that you would willingly drive a tank over it, but you'd still sink. Why? Although you've got loads of faith, the thing you are putting your faith in is weak. Conversely, you can stand by a lake frozen over with such thick ice that they are holding a tank race across it! Yet you cross it gingerly with a rope around your waist and your life insurance policy in your hand. Naturally the ice holds your weight – but why? It isn't to do with the amount of faith you have, but the thing in which you put it.

So if your faith is more akin to Homer Simpson's than Billy Graham's, remember that it's not about how much you've got but where you place it that counts.

Continental

C.S. Lewis said, 'Faith is the art of holding on to things your reason has accepted, in spite of your changing moods.' No matter how you feel today, God still loves the socks off you! That's being sure, that's being certain.

Coffee

'I can promise you this. If you had faith no larger than a mustard seed, you could tell this mountain to move from here to there. And it would. Everything would be possible for you' (Matthew 17:20).

Orange Juice
Your eyes are like a window for your body. When they are good, you have all the light you need. But when your eyes are bad, everything is dark. If the light inside you is dark, you are in the dark. *(MATTHEW 6:22)*

WATCH WHAT YOU WATCH

The Big Breakfast
If you stand in the entrance hall of BBC Broadcasting House in London's Portland Place, you'll read this inscription.

To Almighty God this shrine of the arts, music and literature is dedicated by the first Governors in the year of our Lord 1931, John Reith being Director General. It is their prayer that good seed sown will produce a good harvest, that everything offensive to decency and hostile to peace will be expelled, and that the nation will incline its ear to those things which are lovely, pure and of good report and thus pursue the path of wisdom and virtue.

If some of the BBC's heads of programming reread this inscription then the programmes they commission might change drastically. What we watch and what we listen to affects the way we live our lives.

If our eyes and, I presume, our ears are the gateways to our souls, then we need to place a crack team of security guards around them. Take stock of the late-night TV you watch, the Internet sites you visit and the certificates on the movies you rent. They could turn off the light inside you!

Continental
Solomon's challenge is 'Carefully guard your thoughts, because they are the source of true life' (Proverbs 4:23). Maybe that's because if we don't monitor what comes into them they will become dark, full of 'evil thoughts, vulgar deeds, stealing, murder, unfaithfulness in marriage, greed, meanness, deceit, indecency, envy, insults, pride and foolishness' (Mark 7:21–2).

Coffee
Make the Psalmist's prayer your prayer today: 'Take away my foolish desires, and let me find life by walking with you' (Psalm 119:37). Amen!

Orange Juice

If any of you need wisdom, you should ask God, and it will be given to you. God is generous and won't correct you for asking. But when you ask for something, you must have faith and not doubt.

(JAMES 1:5-7)

YOU'VE GOT MAIL

The Big Breakfast

Subj: Re: Prayer
Date: AD 50 13:23:07 standard time
From: James@Jerusalem.freechurchserve.co.nt
(James, brother of Jesus)
To: Twelvetribes@jol.com

Greetings … Blah, blah, blah,. Thanks for the recent emails. Sorry for the delay in replying but Peter spilt communion wine all over my keyboard again. Listen, I know this Christian life stuff is often a struggle. I mean, I'm family and it still baffles me at times. Being a believer doesn't exempt you from the trials and temptations of life.

If you really have no idea how to handle the next family crisis, or your donkey has failed its MOT again, then talk to the Governor. He's never let me down, always dead keen to help. You won't have to twist his arm into helping out, he'll muck in and sort it out and won't make you feel a right idiot for asking in the first place. So ask the big man boldly, and believe it from me – it's as good as done! You can get him direct at jehovah@billgatesofheaven.org.

Continental

John Donne, the sixteenth-century bishop and poet, summed up my prayer life when he said, 'I throw myself down in my chamber, and I call in, and invite God and his angels thither, and when they are there, I neglect God and his angels for the noise of a fly or the rattling of a coach.'

Coffee

'Ask, and you will receive. Search, and you will find. Knock, and the door will be opened to you. Everyone who asks will receive' (Matthew 7:7).

Orange Juice

What I want from you is plain and clear: I want your constant love, not your animal sacrifices. I would rather have my people know me than burn offerings to me.

(HOSEA 6:5-6 GNB)

The Big Breakfast

A man came home from work as usual, and met his wife standing in the doorway. 'You don't love me any more,' she barked. 'And what's more, I am going to prove it to you. I am wearing something that I haven't worn for ages – since the end of the Second World War, in fact.' The man made his best guess. The skirt? The shoes? The cardigan? They were all wrong. 'What is it?' he asked in desperation. 'It's the gas mask!' she hissed.

How could he miss something as obvious as a gas mask on his wife's face? How can we miss something as obvious as God's best for us? The prophet Hosea reminds us that the blazingly obvious way for us to love God is with consistency rather than mediocrity. God much prefers a daily relationship with us to the sacrifice of getting up earlier than most people on a Sunday to sit in a pew for an hour.

Recently I met an American basketball team from Chicago. They were telling me about the commitment needed to play basketball at the highest level, and talked about being a 24/7 kind of a person. Dedicating 24 hours a day, seven days a week to your sport. It's that same consistency that heaven's coach demands of us if we are to play well on his team.

Continental

Stop burning those offerings to God in place of burning with a passion to walk his way. He would much rather an honest conversation with you about your fears and your failures than a 'good deed' here and there. It's about real relationship, not false religion.

Coffee

The Living Bible puts this verse even more plainly and clearly. God says, 'I don't want your sacrifices – I want your love; I don't want your offerings – I want you to know me.' What is stopping you knowing him today? Push it aside!

Orange Juice
Each morning you listen to my prayer, as I bring my requests to you and wait for your reply.

(PSALM 5:3)

FACING THE DAWN

The Big Breakfast
There is something quite holy about mornings. I know that some of us would replace the word 'holy' with 'hellish' here, but I'm convinced that there is something very precious about how we start our days. I think we miss out if we start them in a frantic rush or if we are still wiping sleep from our eyes at lunchtime.

I went for a run this morning. I did lots of thinking, seemingly without trying, and then completed the exercise with a hot, reviving shower. What a great way to start a day. How do you set yourself up for the day ahead? The author Ken Gire in his book *The Reflective Life* recounts how the Native American begins each morning.

In the life of an Indian ... his daily devotions were more necessary to him than daily food. He wakes at daybreak, puts on his moccasins, and steps down to the water's edge. Here he throws handfuls of clear, cold water into his face ... He then stands strong before the advancing dawn, facing the sun as it dances upon the horizon, and offers his unspoken orison.

How important are your daily devotions? How are you facing the advancing dawn today?

Continental
Notice the way the Psalmist starts his day. He talks to God, lays his requests before him and then ... waits. No action, no giving God a hand by trying to sort it through himself. He just waits ... expectantly. Now that's real adventure.

Coffee
'I am a barbarously early riser ... I love the empty, silent, dewy, cobwebby hours' (C.S. Lewis, 1958). Miss these moments and you will miss out.

Orange Juice
Nothing on earth is more beautiful than the morning sun. Even if you live to a ripe old age you should try to enjoy each day.

(ECCLESIASTES 11:7-8)

TODAY'S THE DAY

The Big Breakfast
Are you old enough to remember the Stingray puppets? The sixties American voiceover always promised us that 'anything could happen in the next half-hour'. Problem is, it never really did; it was always so predictable. You just knew that no matter how desperate the situation, the little wooden puppets would save the world. This predictability eventually made the show boring for me.

My heart breaks as I meet the predictable people in life who never seem to 'enjoy each day' but endure it with a cancerous bitterness. I recently met a bus driver who had once hated his job with a passion and showed it by moaning daily to the endless streams of people who took a ride with him. Then he found Jesus, and life had a new perspective. He never gave up his job – he wasn't able to. Instead, he turned his bus into a temple. He took pleasure in greeting everyone with a smile, even on the rainiest of days. He went the extra mile to help the elderly or the mums with kids. He even won the bus company's driver of the year competition.

The way to enjoy each day is to find God in everything. Your task today is to turn your workplace into a temple, so that when you sit down for your evening meal you can say, 'I have really enjoyed today.'

Continental
As we 'enjoy each day' it's worth remembering Os Guinness's advice: 'Christ-centred heroism does not need to be noticed or publicized. The greatest deeds are done before the audience of one, and that is enough.'

Coffee
Choose to walk away from predictability and to enjoy each day, starting with this one!

Orange Juice

Can't you stick it out with me a single hour? Stay alert; be in prayer so you don't wander into temptation without even knowing you're in danger …

(MATTHEW 26:41 THE MESSAGE)

IT'S GOOD TO TALK

The Big Breakfast

My life feels like one big conversation sometimes. I have days where I go from meeting to meeting, with telephone calls in between. Even in the car, I find myself using the time to make calls on the mobile phone. So I never seem to find the time to stop and reflect unless I deliberately plan it in. Yesterday was one of the those mind-bending, meeting-after-meeting days. I had an hour's car journey early morning and, as usual, I listened to the radio for the latest news and then went to make some urgent calls. It was at that moment that a 'shepherd's warning' red sky burst through the windscreen and ignited something deep in my soul.

It seemed an age since I'd had more than a grabbed conversation with God. It's tough at the best of times when you work for a boss you can't see. It's even harder when you never get round to talking stuff through with him. I switched the phone and the radio off and began to talk … and talk … and talk. I don't know who had missed the other more – me or God.

Switch off what distracts you today and switch back on to God, even if it's been months or years since you last spoke.

Continental

Temptation is far easier to overcome and danger far easier to avoid when prayer is important to our daily routine. Join me in the struggle of not letting our service for God take precedent over our worship of God.

Coffee

Jesus went on to say to his dozy disciples, 'There is a part of you that is eager, ready for anything in God. But there is another part of you that's as lazy as an old dog sleeping by the fire.' Which part will you work on today?

Orange Juice
You have turned my sorrow into joyful dancing. No longer am I sad and wearing sackcloth.

(PSALM 30:11)

DANCE INTO THE LIGHT

The Big Breakfast
God's double whammy! Sorrow into line dancing and sackcloth into Calvin Kleins!

He doesn't just remove your shame, he takes you down to his heavenly Retail Outlet Store and he kits you out with a brand new set of party gear. He doesn't just dry your tears, he puts the kind of smile back on your face that reaches right down to your feet and makes them dance. That's what's so precious about God. No half measures, no naked shame, no 'well-I'll-let-you-off–this-time…'

He always adds his divine Vanish Stain Remover to our garments grimed with guilt and shame. He promises to wash away all the dirt of our tears of pain and failure, and he always delivers on that promise, wash after wash after wash.

Praise is often described in the Bible as a sacrifice (Romans 12:1–2). It's tough to say thank you when your heart is breaking. But allowing the authentic sound of worship to rise up from deep within your soul brings a freedom that doesn't ignore the pain but sings in spite of it – freedom to smile again, to dance and to leave the past behind, freedom to hold your head up high and walk once more, sure of one thing: that in God's eyes the verdict still remains 'not guilty!'

Continental
An old 1936 Irving Berlin song was made popular again by a recent TV advert for life insurance. I like its almost holy arrogance. 'There may be trouble ahead, but while there's moonlight and love and romance, let's face the music and dance.'

Coffee
The Message gives this verse a great street feel. 'You did it: you changed wild lament into whirling dance; you ripped off my black mourning band and decked me with wildflowers.' Dance with God this day.

Orange Juice
Even though I walk through the valley of the shadow of death, I will fear no evil, for you are with me; your rod and your staff, they comfort me.

(PSALM 23:4 NIV)

A BREATH OF HOPE

The Big Breakfast
Last night a good friend died. She was my age and left a husband and three young children behind. Maybe you too can relate to the kind of grief that losing someone you love brings. Maybe, like me, your mind is full of unanswered questions and your heart numb with pain. I want you to know that the first tears to fall in your hurt were the ones that ran down your heavenly Father's cheeks.

I read the *Narnia Chronicles* long before I became a Christian. I never saw the parallel to the Christian life back then, but I do now. As I scrabble around for just an ounce of hope, Lewis's words seem very appropriate for me this morning:

Aslan said softly, 'Now the term is over: the holidays have begun. The dream has ended: this is the morning … And for us this is the end of all the stories … but for them it was only the beginning of the real story. All their life in this world … had only been the cover and the title page: now at last they were beginning Chapter One of the Real Story: in which every chapter is better than the one before.'

There is hope. Great hope. There always is with a God who has beaten the power of death.

Continental
My soul looked to Psalm 23 for comfort and I noticed something I hadn't seen before. It wasn't the valley of death we go through, but the valley of the *shadow* of death. You only get a shadow when there is a blazing light to create it. Right there in our darkest moments, God's dazzling light is our guide. He is with us and he will comfort us.

Coffee
Rejoice in the defiant hope of this divine declaration:

Death swallowed by triumphant Life! Who got the last word, oh, Death? Oh, Death, who's afraid of you now? (1 Corinthians 15:55 The Message)

Orange Juice

The poor have a hard life, but being content is as good as an *endless feast.*

(PROVERBS 15:15)

MADE FOR ANOTHER WORLD

The Big Breakfast

I have often wondered what heaven will be like, probably because one day I am going to spend quite a long time there. I remember one preacher explaining eternity as a huge granite mountain. Each year a little bird would pay a visit, perch on its lofty peak and peck once before it flew off, not to return for another twelve months. When that granite mountain is eventually worn down to dust – that will be like 'day one' of eternity. Mind-bending, isn't it? One thing I do know is that heaven is not just a future hope but a present reality. Eternal life begins now, not when we die. The 'endless feast' has already begun.

While working with a missions team in a church near Larnaca in Cyprus, we were taken out for a traditional Greek meal. Talk about endless feast – we had course after course. I gave up counting after 36! We even stopped a few times to conga with the waiters around the restaurant and out into the high street. It was a most memorable event and it certainly cheered my heart.

Enjoy the feast today. The succulent tastes of a hope that will never disappoint, a friend who will never leave and a peace that is felt but can never be explained.

Continental

I once shared a feast with a poor family in a foreign country. Their generosity was outstanding, yet their food and table manners were questionable. Everybody but me tucked in eagerly. My host whispered in my ear, 'Duncan, if pride stops you eating you will go hungry.' Dive into God's banquet today. Don't be shy or you'll starve.

Coffee

In *Mere Christianity* C.S. Lewis writes, 'If I find in myself a desire which no experience in this world can satisfy, the most probable explanation is that I was made for another world.' Take a moment to set your soul towards heaven.

Orange Juice

Don't be fooled, my dear friends. Every good and perfect gift comes down from the Father who created all the lights in the heavens. *He is always the same and never makes dark shadows by changing.*

(JAMES 1:16–17)

CHANGING TIMES

The Big Breakfast

Of one thing we can all be certain – constant change is here to stay. Our society seems to change faster than a McLaren F1 pit stop. It only seems a breath away that the web was just something Mrs Spider lived in. We used to swap phone numbers at parties, then it was mobiles and email addresses. Vinyl records are now only seen at jumble sales. Compact discs are giving way to mini disks, while VHS video is about to exit stage left in preference to DVD. When I was at school, teachers were stamping out such discipline problems as talking in class or running in the corridors. Nowadays it's more likely to be problems of truancy or drug and alcohol abuse.

I am increasingly convinced that in this sea awash with constant change, people are desperately searching out the dry ground of certainty that previous generations seemed to enjoy. That makes our faith increasingly relevant today as we proclaim a God who 'is always the same and never makes dark shadows by changing'.

Continental

'Jesus Christ never changes! He is the same yesterday, today, and for ever' (Hebrews 13:8). In other words, he loves you no more or less than he did the day he hung on the cross for you.

Coffee

Change is not all bad. My wife, a nurse herself, smiled as I read her *The Duty of a Nurse in 1887*. 'Nurses in good standing with the director will be given an evening off each week for courting purposes or two evenings a week if you go regularly to church. Any nurse who gets her hair done at a beauty shop or frequents dance halls will give the director good reason to suspect her worth and integrity.' It's good that some things change, don't you think?

Orange Juice

The man in charge drank some of the water that had now turned into wine ... 'The best wine is always served first. Then after the guests have had plenty, the other wine is served. *But you have saved the best until last!*'

(JOHN 2:9–10)

PARTY POOPER

The Big Breakfast

This was Jesus' first miracle. If you take the time to read the whole story you'll understand that Jesus doesn't gatecrash this party: he's on the invited list, his name's on the door (John 2:2). I find that fascinating. You see, many people think that Jesus was a party pooper, but no one invites party poopers to parties. And he proved it by turning the rancid water from the six stone foot-washing jars into a cheeky little number from God's own personal vineyard. And it wasn't just a bottle or two, not even a case ... oh no ... Jesus demonstrates again the extravagant nature of heaven by supplying this flagging party with around thirty gallons of the good stuff.

The horrified servants look on as Ben the spotty Saturday boy is given the first glass drawn from the water jars and ordered to take it to the master at the top table. Surely he'll spit it out, and throw them out. The room hushes, the word has gone round. Jesus smiles as the master sups ... and sups, his only comment: 'You have saved the best until last.'

As I write and you read, I wonder whether heaven's switchboard is making a divine connection between my words and your soul today. He's saved the best till now!

Continental

I have often conducted the weddings of people who thought they would never find a soulmate or prayed for people who have waited patiently for the right job. I can recall laughing with people who have looked back on where they would have been without a God who knew what was best for them and had saved it till now.

Coffee

John goes on to record the impact of this first and most extravagantly controversial of miracles. 'Jesus showed his glory, and his disciples put their faith in him' (John 2:11). How about you?

Orange Juice

Jesus … shouted, 'Lazarus, come out!' The man who had been dead came out. His hands and feet were wrapped with strips of burial cloth, and a cloth covered his face. Jesus then told the people, '*Untie him and let him go.*'

(JOHN 11:43–4)

FUNERAL CHAOS

The Big Breakfast

Can you imagine turning up to a funeral with Jesus, four days late, only for him to say that the corpse may be a touch yellow but he's not dead, he's just having a little doze? And that Jesus will give him the loudest wake-up call he's ever likely to hear (John 11:11)?

Jesus tells the people to remove the stone from the tomb. The dead man's sister gently suggests that he might pong a bit. Jesus replies that they might like to trust him as he is the resurrection and the life and therefore is best qualified to deal with this one, thank you very much.

Jesus calls Lazarus out by name. The only sound that's heard as the mummified figure of Lazarus appears in the doorway to the tomb is the thud of the disciples' jaws as they hit the dusty Middle Eastern ground. Jesus has to tell the boys to unwrap him and let him go!

What are the grave-clothes that have tied you up for so long? Your gender doesn't fit, so you have to keep quiet and make the tea. You've been told that you are too old for this game now, or maybe it's that you're too young and can't be trusted with that kind of responsibility.

Continental

Hear the Master's loud voice calling out to you today, 'Take off those grave-clothes. Don't be bound any more. Be free … be completely free.'

Coffee

The shortest verse in the Bible is part of the Lazarus story. Just two simple words – 'Jesus wept.' Only nine letters, but you could fill a library with their meaning. How does the Saviour react when he sees the grave-clothes strangling his life out of you? Jesus weeps.

Orange Juice
Jesus wept.

(JOHN 11:35 NIV)

TEARS FROM HEAVEN

The Big Breakfast
And the tears are still rolling to this day …

He weeps over my ability to preach truth with my mouth and practise heresy with my life.

He weeps over the bride he adores who is so often heartbroken and heartless.

He weeps over communities that choose death not life, houses not homes, clean air not clean minds.

He weeps over a society that has gained possessions but lost values.

He weeps over people who understand the far reaches of outer space but have neglected their own inner space, who have beaten disease but not prejudice.

He weeps over generations who have written more but have learned less, who have developed disposable nappies along with their throw-away morality.

He weeps over a race that has faster modems but less communication, that builds worlds of leisure but has lost the art of having fun, that has more experts but more problems.

Let your heart be broken today with the things that break the heart of God. Let the tears fall.

Continental
T.S. Eliot once wrote:

*The desert is not only remote in southern tropics
The desert is not only around the corner
The desert is squeezed in the tube train next to you
The desert is in the heart of your brother.*

Coffee
When Jesus came closer and could see Jerusalem, he cried and said, 'Today your people don't know what will bring them peace! Now it is hidden from them. Jerusalem, the time will come when your enemies … close in on you from every side … because you did not see that God had come to save you' (Luke 19:41–4).

Orange Juice

God did this because he wanted you Gentiles to understand his wonderful and glorious mystery. And the mystery is that Christ lives in you, and he is your hope of sharing in God's glory.

(COLOSSIANS 1:27)

CLOSER THAN YOU THINK

The Big Breakfast

I have to admit to being a bit of a *Star Trek* fan, though it's really only the old 1960s series that gets me switching on the TV set. I love the dramatic music, the rubber aliens, the painted polystyrene sets. My heart always breaks for the newest member of the landing party: it's clear that the alien slime will get them first and that they're never coming back. After the programme I go to bed dreaming of a fictitious world where we can flip open a communicator (that looks mysteriously like a woman's make-up compact) and get Scotty to beam us anywhere we fancy.

Just imagine that fiction became reality for one moment. Imagine Scotty pushing up his faders and beaming you right into the courtyards of heaven. Do you think you would be closer to God than you are now? Not according to the apostle Paul. The mystery that was once a secret is now revealed – 'Christ lives in you'. You are just as close to him now as you would be holding an audience with God in heaven. Maybe there wouldn't be as many distractions then, but remember this truth: God has taken up residence deep within you. So you don't need to come into his presence today. You never left it!

Continental

If we have all fallen short of the glory of God, is there any hope of ever reaching it? Answer: yes – 'Christ lives in you, and he is your hope of sharing in God's glory'. The only hope you have of reaching the standard God sets is if the indwelling Christ meets it for you. It has to be an inside job.

Coffee

The Message manages to put this verse so bluntly and memorably: 'The mystery in a nutshell is just this: Christ is in you, therefore you can look forward to sharing in God's glory. It's that simple.'